Advance
'A Fistful
Memories of Jawhar

"You had shared a gem with me back in 2016: 'A Fistful of My Sky: Memories of Jawhar.' This beautiful treasure of a young doctor who is embarking on a meaningful journey is so thoughtfully strung by his experiences, reflections and life's lessons gained through wisdom over the years. I have started to read this book again and the feeling of wanting to soak in every bit of learning is so surreal. At this point, through this book, I'm also realising how I have changed over the years. My perception of things back then versus now has significantly broadened. This self-discovery is amazing! I'm so grateful to you for sharing this gem. And wishing I get a few more glimpse of your life's journey.

– Beena Salla.
Organisation Psychologist.

'.....What a write up...could picture every incident...every event ...that happened in the 6 months. Marvellous..i just could not stop reading ...just wanted to know what's next ??? Congratulations to you too for being a part of this profession. Sadly our system does fail for the poor strata of society. After all the efforts put in by the team to face situations so helpless ....it sets one thinking on the deeper issues of life. Loved the book!!

– Friend of Dr. Hiroo Motwani.

'Fantastic .....It's like a screenplay. ..Felt like I was reliving my entire experience there...You described the subtle intricacies very well... and painstakingly elaborated.'

– Dr. Salauddin Dadan.
Physician.

Advance Praise for 'A Fistful of My Sky: Memories of Jawhar'

Overall, I loved it. It's definitely a page turner. It is raw but that is where its beauty lies. The way you have narrated everything, from beginning to end, character after character, plot after plot. This is what I'd call simplicity at its best.

It had been a really long time since i read something good, you know, something you can connect to right from the very beginning.

I was engrossed in reading and not once did i think that it will come to an end, it was only when i was down to the last 5 pages did i realise that i won't have anything further to read.

This book, believe me or not, is going to be in my top 5 'must reads'. I hope it gets published soon and the whole world gets to experience what you did in those 4 months.

The book was an eye opener. It touched my heart by its simplicity and straightforwardness. There wasn't any drama, it wasnt dragged at all and everything was crisp and to the point. The book was an amazing read. It's the first time i have finished a book from start to finish in a day. Loved each and every word of it.

– Pritika Seth.
Chartered Accountant.

It is entirely unfair that someone with such a strong aptitude for the sciences, can also write so beautifully. Your flair for using the most evocative descriptors brings your experience in Jawhar alive. The anecdotes were, in some ways so painful to read, and ever so poignant. Also, the book brings to light many issues about the medical system that need to be corrected. Not only can non-medical folk such as myself be moved, I'm sure it would even move a stone-heart medico who reads the hearttouching stories within these covers. I feel it should be mandatory reading for medical students in India. It will nurture empathy. It is also a testament to the human spirit, of the doctors and of the patients. It could also lend itself to the screen.

– Sonia Hirdramani.
Investor, Writer and Bibliophile. Sri Lanka.

Advance Praise for 'A Fistful of My Sky: Memories of Jawhar'

I finished reading it, and I absolutely loved it! I thought it was so touching, and I was so moved by each of the stories of the patients. I was especially moved by Dhavali's story, it was heart-breaking, but to see her recovery was so inspiring. For me, the most powerful parts of the book were the relationships you formed with the patients as well as your colleagues. I think you are a beautiful writer, and I felt really attached to the characters and the story - I didn't want it to end!

I also think it is a valuable book as it tells the story of an overlooked village which has such an important story to tell, your book will help make sure they are never forgotten.

– Sonia Jordan.
Aspiring Journalist and Writer. UK.

CONGRATULATIONS for a superbly written memoir. All the case studies were written with such detail and I am amazed at your ability to remember so well.

I may not have known so much of what you have written, but even now I can say again, how proud I am of you, and your sense of social responsibility. The anecdotes in every aspect were very touching and poignant.

There is a lesson even in the final few lines. That we should try and keep to our promises... that we should try and live our lives with keen awareness. May your writing inspire younger men and women in your profession.

Well done!

– C. C. Maniar.
Corporate Consultant.

A Fistful of My Sky: Memories of Jawhar

Dr. Anand Gokani, MD.

ZB

ZORBA BOOKS

ZORBA BOOKS

Published by Zorba Books, May 2024
Website: www.zorbabooks.com
Email: info@zorbabooks.com
Author Name: Dr. Anand Gokani, MD.
Copyright ©: Dr. Anand Gokani, MD.

Title: A Fistful of My Sky: Memories of Jawhar

Printbook ISBN: 978-93-5896-449-3
Ebook ISBN: 978-93-5896-928-3

Zorba Books Pvt. Ltd. (opc)
Sushant Arcade,
Next to Courtyard Marriot,
Sushant Lok 1, Gurgaon – 122009, India

Printed by Manipal Technologies Limited
A1 & A2 Shivalli Industrial Area Manipal Udupi, Karnataka – 57610

Dedication

Dedicated to the Adivasis of Jawhar who taught me about
Resilience, Simplicity and the Art of accepting one's
Fate with Equanimity.

Contents

Contents

Contents

Preface

Dr. Farokh E. Udwadia MD. FRCP.

THIS BOOK IS A SOUL-stirring, breath-taking account of a medical internship lasting six months, served by Dr. Anand Gokani and his young colleagues in rural India. The name of this village cum small township is Jawhar, situated in the Thane district of Maharashtra. These young, fresh graduate interns were based in a primitive village hospital serving this poverty-stricken district.

This book is a saga of courage, determination, professionalism, compassion, dedication and service shown by these doctors to the poor, destitute and needy. I feel amazed at the range of problems they tackled so successfully in primitive conditions, helped by just a few nurses and supporting staff. There is a poignancy in the author's account of the illnesses encountered among the Adivasis living in this village and in the surrounding areas.

The book also pictures the heart of rural India --- the heart that bleeds but continues to beat. One is aware of this, but it is different when one actually experiences it, as these young doctors did, during their internship. One is deeply moved by the stark poverty of the Adivasis and the other poor living in and around Jawhar-- the malnutrition, the disease, the lack of shelter, the miserable living conditions and the struggle for their daily existence. Yet, one is even more struck by their courage, their endurance, their faith, and their simple, yet overwhelmingly genuine, gratitude to the doctors for the help they rendered.

This encounter, of the young doctors with the poor and needy in India, must have certainly left an indelible impression on their minds and hearts. They must have learnt that medicine is not about knowing, treating or even curing, but about compassion, caring and healing.

This book is well-written, the sentences short and sweet, the style racy. I started reading it in the late evening and could not put it down till I finished it late in the night. This charming book should be read by all medical students, interns, residents and doctors, particularly by the young, who are to embark or have just embarked into their professional careers.

Introduction

If I have to look back and zero in on the most challenging phase of my life, it would be the time I served at a village called Jawhar during my internship. We had just graduated and were now proud that we could add the prefix to our names......

Dr. Anand Gokani, MBBS.! We had worked hard for it, and it felt like a suitable culmination of a major phase in our lives, where we had sacrificed so much to get to where we were. It was a moment to celebrate and most of us were in that spirit.

The lobby outside the Department of Medicine was abuzz with activity as the students started assembling for their Internship allotments. The internship would extend for a year, wherein we served six months at an Urban centre and six months at a Rural centre. I had opted to serve at the JJ Hospital in the first six months and then, serve at Jawhar in the next six months. This decision was heavily criticised by my friends, who had opted for 'light' centres for rural internships, as it could then be treated as a holiday. I had been the black sheep to have opted for the most difficult centre. But I had my reasons.......

I was in a quandary......In the forthcoming year, I had to choose between Medicine and Surgery, as my speciality for the Master's degree. Though I loved the excitement of Surgery and it's attendant rewards, I was also aware of the serious vision problem that I had, precluding me from fine work which was so necessary in good surgery. I still wanted to give it a go, and the best place to experiment with my surgical skill and aptitude was at Jawhar. I had heard that, at the hospital in Jawhar, we were given a free lease to do whatever we wanted to, and that gave us the opportunity to experience doing surgeries of all sorts, albeit under the guidance of a senior practitioner. I didn't want to give up that chance no matter what my friends said.

So Jawhar it was......And what follows in the subsequent pages, is an honest, unexpurgated account of life in the remote Adivasi village where we spent six months treating the poorest of the poor, the marginalised, the neglected and forgotten humanity. The reason I share this experience is that, even after more than 40 years, the memories of that experience are crystal clear and, even after having been all over the advanced world of Medicine, seen the best and worked in challenging and difficult situations, I still feel that the work we did there gave us more gratification, more fulfilment and more joy. The simple, uncomplicated lives of the rustic poor, the generosity amidst abject poverty, the resilience and tenacity in times of adversity and the calm equanimity to accept any fate and to move on, are qualities that I saw there and learnt for myself. No other experience has taught me as much as those six months and, today, I want to share them with you.

Prologue

It was the 15th of July, 1981. The date on which my rural internship was to commence. Six months of the urban internship had ended yesterday, and my heart was filled with both, anticipation for the new experience and trepidation for the completely alien atmosphere we would be working in. Having dwelt in the city all my life, the thought of living in a primitive village was a source of tremendous anxiety. Urban internship had been a great experience. We had worked long hours at the hospital and had actually put our hands in the blood and gore. It had been a baptism by fire.

Assisting in surgeries, doing minor procedures in the wards, conducting blood tests, urine tests, stool tests in the very basic side-room lab, and helping manage all kinds of emergencies and routine, planned work. We had spent two months in the Surgical wards, two months in the Medicine wards, and two months in the Gynaecology and Obstetrics wards. Having completed this rotation, we had been imparted ample opportunity to experience each faculty, and this had raised the level of our confidence to handle disease significantly. As urban internship drew to a close our apprehension began to increase. We were heading for a very big change in our lives.

My colleagues in Jawhar were five other class mates......Drs. Hiroo Motwani, Yogendra Sanghvi, Hemant Painter, Salauddin Dadan, and Abdul Razzak Syed. A motley mix of young doctors with one thing in common......Dedication. The dedication and the wide-eyed enthusiasm to explore, experiment, and to plunge into any adventure headlong, with no fear or hesitation.

Prologue

We had planned on meeting at the Bombay Central Bus Station at 5.45 am to travel together to Jawhar. Heavy rains and strong winds lashed the city all night. Amidst the wetness and humidity, we found our way to the bus terminus. The bus depot was a depressing place, ill-lit by tubelights placed non-strategically, and extremely crowded with all kinds of people wanting to travel to various, diverse destinations. There were farmers, labourers, petty businessmen, brokers, some families and of course, our group of young doctors.

The rains didn't do much to alleviate the filth and squalor within the bus. The windows being shut, the atmosphere in the bus smelt musty, a heady mix of body odour, sweat, dampness and bidi smoke. In the days before tobacco was banned in public places, there were always some uncouth people who would periodically light up a bidi and smoke it inside the bus with impunity.

Smoke, stench, stale air and the incessant din of rain beating on the roof of the bus were the first moments of our rural internship. A lot more was in store for all of us!

1. The First Bus Ride

At precisely 6.15 am the bus driver jumped into his seat and the conductor gave out the last call for the stragglers to board the bus, shouting into no particular direction, just hollering over the prevailing din. The bus rattled to a start and there was this chorus that arose from the passengers, heralding the start of the journey. We were seated in the first row facing forwards. The bus rattled its way out of the terminus, hooting the endless stream of humanity out of its way. Bombay Central, Dadar, Matunga, Sion, and then onto the Eastern Express Highway. At this point the bus picked up speed and the rattling increased. Despite the smell and sound, despite the discomfort, the rhythm lulled us to sleep. Most of the passengers seemed to have shut their eyes and drifted off already. After two and a half hours of this rattle fest we reached Bhivandi, known as the textile town. It was the hub of the power loom industry manufacturing artificial silk. Many of the passengers alighted here and a few boarded. For the onward journey the bus was less crowded and hence more comfortable.

Beyond Bhivandi, the bus began its ascent into the hills and into tribal territory. The terrain changed from an urban concrete jungle to a more rustic, natural landscape. The change was exhilarating. The rains had cleansed the foliage and there was greenery all around. Tall trees, the smell of wet earth and a cool breeze prevailed as we approached Wada. Thereafter the ghats commenced. The bus slowed down. Labouring up the steep slopes of this hilly region. The rattling of the bus, interspersed by the clanging of shifting gears and the occasional toot-toot from the hooter to warn animals and people alike, were the only sounds that pervaded our senses. We passed many small villages as we wound our way to Jawhar.

The monsoon had transformed the landscape to an extravagance of green. The trees were tall and lush, the shrubs varied and innumerable. The character of the people had changed suddenly after passing Wada. The urban demeanour changed to a rustic innocence and simplicity. The road was pretty, though pot-holed, but not really that bad. The scenery beyond Wada was breathtaking. The beauty of Nature, the peace, the changed character of the people, made me forget about my forthcoming ordeal for the moment.

2. What Ordeal?

Why did I call this an ordeal? This was ostensibly the finest period of my life, yet this journey was leading me to an ordeal that made me very uncomfortable. The plan was that any four of us would stay at the centre at a given time and the others could accommodate their free time accordingly. So I had decided to take the first two months off and return to work for the remaining four months at a stretch. In keeping with this plan, I was to report for duty with the others, and then, quietly slip off the next morning. I had plans of travelling overseas for some exams and for some travel. I was so looking forwards to this trip, but my biggest fear was of being penalised for my illicit absence from my internship posting. What if?......A thousand 'what ifs' plagued my mind and tormented me as the bus wended its way to Jawhar. The conflicting emotions of apprehension, fear, guilt and anxiety, against the excitement of a new experience, were inundating my mind in every possible way.

3. Jawhar!

At 11am the bus rolled into this little hilltop town. Narrow lanes with a rustic charm, people walking around, small shops lining the road, low houses with sloping roofs, rain-splashed windowpanes, muddy water filling potholes, an occasional cyclist ringing his bell incessantly, making his way around people seemingly oblivious of his presence, a hen scampering across the street, stray dogs, muddy and hungry looking, foraging in an open garbage heap by the side of the road......And there was a freshness in the air devoid of toxic fumes and dust, a freshness that has to be smelled, felt and experienced. That was Jawhar!

Jawhar was a small town but an important principality of the district as it was the seat of administration, education and health for the entire region. The market place was crowded as all town centres are. The main landmark was a statue of Mahatma Gandhi in the main market, that precinct being known as Gandhi Chowk.

Patangsha Cottage Hospital, the hospital where we were to spend the next six months, was about a kilometre from the bus station and atop a hillock, majestically looking down on the rest of the town. The architecture of the hospital building was royal. White domes supported by black stone walls lending it a monumental and regal charm. This hospital was built by the Maharajah of Jawhar, from the Mukne family.

Shielded by an umbrella against the incessant drizzle of rain, we slowly walked up the hill, approaching the hospital with a sense of awe and anticipation.

4. The Cottage Hospital

It was a five minute walk to the hospital. As we drew closer, we saw the hectic activity of patients and their relatives at the threshold of the building. Amidst this were the familiar faces...our friends ...the out-going interns. Our friends gave us a rousing welcome.

We were ushered into the hospital and taken through the building in a jiffy. We were quickly shown the location of the male ward, the female ward, the maternity ward and the labour room. These were adjoining an infrequently used main operation theatre (MOT) and an over-used minor operation theatre. There was also the out- patient department which was at the front of the hospital. This is where we would be seeing all our patients every day. There were also the Chief Medical Officer's office and residence and the pharmacy. That comprised the precincts of the hospital. We were to discover every area in detail in the course of the next six months.

The nurses were looking out of their room to see who the new incumbents were and waved to us tentatively awaiting a more formal introduction. The elderly pharmacist with his young son were at the door of the pharmacy driven by the same curiosity. In just over a minute we had seen the hospital and the staff with whom we would be spending so much of our next six months.

5. Home Away from Home

Behind the hospital was a small square building, possibly 20 feet by 20 feet, which was going to serve as our residence for the next six months. Badly in need of a coat of paint, the building had weather-beaten walls with chipped plaster and a flat roof. Three steps at the entrance and we were in a small anteroom with a table and four chairs, ostensibly dining room. We entered the room and, in one look, took in the rest of the house. There were two small rooms with three cots each, and one common toilet facility and a small kitchenette. This was our home away from home.

We put our bags down in the bedroom randomly selecting our space in the small tenement. Hemant Kotwal and Shriram Upadhyaya, interns from our class, who had already finished their posting, were going to hand over charge to us today and leave by the evening bus.

"You guys must be hungry? Did you have any breakfast this morning?" Hemant asked.

"Just some biscuits," someone replied diffidently.

"There is still some time for lunch. Would you guys like some tea?"

"Would love some! Who'll make?"

After this long and rickety journey, the rain falling incessantly, and the feeling of dampness, mixed with a tinge of fatigue, made the idea of a warm drink all the more welcome. Just the right setting for a hot cup of tea.

"Okay. You guys relax. I'll just call Vahini in a moment." Hemant shot off to call Sudha Vahini. She was someone we would depend on heavily in the months to come. She arrived and got about the task of making tea for us.

The hot cup of tea infused us with renewed energy. We sat around, talking for a while, getting a first hand, ball-to-ball account on life at the hospital. We were being filled in on all things good, bad and ugly, as also the people and situations we should beware of. This passage of experiences was vital for us so as to save us embarrassment or trouble during our stint in the village hospital. I was listening intently and trying to absorb the nuances of extreme rural life.

6. Meeting the Chief

Sitting behind his oversized table, this slim, small-built man with long hair, a black moustache slicked with a generous dab of oil, Dr. Dhande was hardly the man we had expected to see as the CMO. He was squeaky clean in his white shirt and white trousers. He was brusque and business-like, maybe in an attempt to dominate from the very start, so as to have an upper hand on us. First, he briefed us about the code of conduct and what our duties would be. Later, he accepted our papers and told us to get acquainted with the hospital, the routine would be explained to us by the out-going interns. After we finished our discussion we realised that he was quite an harmless and simple man and was just putting on an air of authority.

The Patangsha Cottage Hospital had a Chief Medical Officer and an assistant medical officer (AMO).. Dr. A. B. Nisal was the designated CMO, but as he was on leave at that time, we didn't meet him. Instead, we met Dr. Dhande (the AMO), who gave us the first introductory talk. In the future months we were to build a good relationship with both these gentleman.

After the briefing we returned to the room. Drs. Kotwal and Upadhyaya were to leave in the evening as they had obtained their completion certificates and had now passed on the responsibility to us. It was a day of mixed feelings for us. For them it was sadness as they were leaving the place that had given them such profound gratification, and for us, it was a day of apprehension and anticipation.

As dusk set in, the hospital assumed a slightly depressing look. The reason being that the lights were dim and the place was run down. The change from the comforts of an urban home to the hardships of ultra-rustic life was a kind of culture shock. It's not as if we were soft and couldn't manage it. We had, during our urban postings, suffered a lot of hardships and had long working hours, at times working 36-hour shifts. But this was different and remained to be experienced.

Working in a primitive hospital, catering to people who have no means or very frugal means in addition to being poor, illiterate and ignorant of the ways of the world, was a challenge for even the stone-hearted amongst us. We were gradually beginning to realise the trials that we were going to be facing in the forthcoming months.

As the dusk gave way to darkness there was an eerie silence in the neighbourhood. This silence was in sharp contrast to the city's hustle and bustle. We had gotten used to the sounds of traffic, television sets blaring a mix of sounds from different households, and the sounds of people talking till late in the night. In Jawhar, owing to a paucity of electricity, the people had nothing to do after dark and hence every one was asleep early. The only sounds that one could hear were the occasional howl of the village dogs, the croaking of toads, and the buzzing of a million crickets like a kind of tinnitus pervading the atmosphere of the night.

Our worst shock was when we entered the room to sleep. the walls were dotted with a hundred different insects! They were something I had never seen in my life before. In various shapes and sizes, and in the most vivid colours. It was not frightening, it was breathtaking, it was fascinating, it was Nature at its best. We were well protected by the mosquito net, which, if handled carefully, kept the insects out of our sleeping area.

That night, we slept peacefully and woke up fresh and relaxed. I was ready before breakfast, as the plan was that I would leave to go back to Bombay. I would then return in the first week of September. Silently, surreptitiously, unbeknownst to the Medical Officer, I slipped away and disappeared.

7. Summons

After leaving Jawhar surreptitiously, I travelled to England to appear for some examinations and spent 7 weeks there. After returning......

TWO MONTHS LATER....

As I was preparing to return to Jawhar, I received an ominous telegram from the Dean's office. Any communication from the Dean's office is always bad news. I could sense, even before opening that little slip of paper, that some serious trouble was brewing. With trembling hands I opened the envelope. Reading the contents made my heart sink and my feet went cold with fear. "Now I've had it!!" I thought to my self. I will have to deal with this problem forthwith.

I looked at the telegram again, dismayed. It read, "INTERN, ANAND GOKANI, ABSCONDING. NOT REPORTED FOR DUTY. TO MEET DEAN IMMEDIATELY."

Absconding? What a word to use. Like a criminal had jumped the jail wall and disappeared! In hindsight, however, I don't think there could be a better word to describe the act. But.......It made me feel like a criminal and that peeved me no end.

What excuse can I offer?....

What do I say to the Dean?....

That I had gone abroad.... For an holiday?....to write an exam.? To enable me to study abroad?

All these options were illegitimate. We were not allowed to make trips during internship. It was strictly proscribed. We did all this secretly with the connivance of lax medical officers and a weak system which allowed these irregularities to pass unnoticed. Even as I was doing it, I had felt pangs of guilt. That's why the first trip had been an ORDEAL. It was an ordeal of the conscience, knowing that what I was doing was wrong. I had actually left Jawhar like a criminal escaping from confinement. In hindsight, I had ample guidance from my conscience but I had chosen to act otherwise.

"Okay," I told myself, "You have done the deed, now prepare to pay the penalty!"

Now was the time for the reckoning.

Should I go to the Dean and come clean?.... or should I lie and say I was sick or something? Or....Should I just go back to Jawhar and let the Medical Officer deal with the Dean.

All the options were flashing across my mind....some were easy options with possible adverse repercussions later....One option was straight and honest. to just go to the Dean and tell him honestly that I had gone for some time and that I would now return to Jawhar and work there diligently, and give no further cause for complaints. After all the turmoil I thought this was the best option....To go to the Dean and come clean.

The next day....

I went to the Dean's office but was told that the Dean was busy. Dr. Anjanayelu, the Dean, a very learned man and a thorough gentleman, was a stern task master. Facing him was an ordeal for the seasoned brave hearts, I was a mere mortal medical student. I can't describe my relief to learn that he was busy and that I couldn't meet him. His office assistant told me that he had received an intimation from the medical officer of Jawhar's Cottage Hospital regarding my absence and that I didn't have to meet the Dean, I just had to go and report for work. On a personal note, he told me not to worry but that I should join immediately and work sincerely. Extremely relieved, I headed home to pack my bags and leave the next morning for Jawhar.

8. Back to Jawhar

The next morning I boarded the 6.15 bus. The journey was the same. Most of the journey was spent in slumber as the movement of the bus, coupled with nothing to do, lulled me to sleep. On reaching, I made a bee line for the hospital. On arriving, I made for Dr. Dhande's office. He was sitting there and was surprised to see me.

"Where have you been, doctor?"

"Sir, I'm sorry, I went away after reporting for work."

"Where have you been all these days?"

"Sir, I had some personal work to attend to. I'm sorry sir. I'm back now and I promise I won't give you another reason to complain." Having blurted my apology I waited for his response.

"Do you realise that we were worried? You joined and then disappeared without informing me? Do you realise that we are responsible for your safety and well-being whilst you are here? You MUST inform us before going back. It's common courtesy."

This admonition was not going down well with me. It was humiliating at best and I was drowning in guilt and regret. "Yes, Sir. It won't happen again, Sir."

"Okay. Join immediately.......and....don't ever do something like this again or else the consequences will not be good!" His parting admonition for me.

It was enough for me. I was sure I would never in my life do something like this again. "Sir, it has happened for the first and last time. Never again, I promise. I shouldn't have gone without discussing the plan with you. I'm sorry, Sir. I do appreciate your concern. I understand my mistake."

"Okay, go! Your friends will introduce you to the procedures in the hospital and acquaint you with the work and the people who you will work with."

After this deep and abiding admonition I returned to the doctor's quarters with a feeling of remorse and shame. Remorse because I had breached a basic etiquette. I painfully realised his point of view and fully appreciated his concern. I resolved never to ever resort to cowardly behaviour again, however grave the situation may be. The matter was closed after this conversation. I realised, after this encounter, that though Dr. Dhande was such an unimpressive looking man, his looks were utterly misleading. He was full of compassion, concern and care. He had a humane streak despite all his professed strictness. I guess in order to keep us in check that attitude is needed. In the next few months I would be getting to know him much better.

9. Work

It didn't take me long to settle down as I had already been here, albeit for just a day. The memories of that day were vividly imprinted in my mind. The good parts and the bad. My friends were full of stories of the things that they had done in these past two months. I spent the day tagging along with them, getting acquainted with the place and the work. From the next day Hemant Painter and Yogendra Sanghavi were going to return to Bombay for a break as they had worked incessantly during my absence. Hiroo Motwani was going to stay on and Salauddin Dadan was going to join us. The sixth member of the team, Abdul Razzak Syed, had shown no inclination to work and was absent for most of the time save a few brief visits.

The People. Let me start by introducing the people I worked with. They are the ones with whom I have shared the rich adventures of the forthcoming months.

Dr. A. B. Nisal. He was the Chief Medical Officer of the P. Cottage Hospital and had just recently been posted here. He was a gynaecologist by qualification, but I suspect he didn't enjoy his work so much. His forte was public relations. He enjoyed meeting and talking to people, especially those in high places. He left the work to us most of the time, as I was to discover in the course of the next few months. He was a good- natured man, sporting long hair, short in stature and a tad 'filmy' in his style.

Dr. Dhande, the Assistant Medical Officer, already discussed in an earlier chapter. His defining feature was his rock-solid common sense and the twinkle in his eye when he hit upon a practical solution when we were foxed by the books. His supreme skill was in performing vasectomies, the process of sterilising men by tying and disconnecting the vas deferens, the tube that carries sperms from the testes to the urethra. This surgery was then known as the Family Planning Surgery. There were days when we were made to assist him whilst he would do 20-30 such cases in quick succession.

Dr. Ujwala Narde, the anaesthetist attached to our cottage hospital. She was a good-natured, almost innocent lady, who was often the butt of jokes poking fun at her naïveté and coy behaviour. She was talented, with painting being her prime forte. One of her paintings had been put up on the wall in our room too.

The Nurses. There were five nurses on a permanent basis and, over the next few months, they were our sole source of encouragement and support. They were the girls who actually worked in the most primitive conditions but never complained about anything. If they didn't know something they would ask, and if they knew better, they would share with us. Nothing was impossible for them. Together, we would make the most of what we had, or else we would innovate.

There was a senior nurse and midwife, Sister Shringarpure, better known universally as Maushi. She was a frail, elderly lady, small of build, myopic eyes and a caring, gentle demeanour. She was the uncrowned queen of the hospital. People came and people went, but she had remained there and was respected for her experience and her loving nature. She ruled over the nurses. First she would train them, and then when they performed tasks well, she was the first to applaud their efforts.

The next one in seniority was Sister Kadrekar. A tad matronly in appearance, not given to unnecessary talk but always willing to work. She was dependable and did her work very well. There was a lot for us to learn from her. On a personal level, she was shy and took time to open up to us.

The two Sisters Shinde were the younger and more energetic girls. They were quiet but did their work diligently. The smaller

Sister Shinde was really diminutive and often had us wondering as to where, in her small frame, did she pack the energy and strength to do a 8- or 12-hour shift. She had an endearing polite manner, and at the end of four months all of us had a sort of protective feeling about her.

Lastly, Sister Neelima Malusare, the vivacious, bright and extremely hardworking girl. She had a flair and style that was instantly attractive.

They all worked hard and were a very good support system we could depend on. The team was further augmented by a pharmacist, Mr. Vashani. He was an elderly gent who lived on the premises with his wife and young son. The son was about 11 years old. Vashani was soft-spoken and well-mannered.

Haribhau, the 'man for all seasons', was the general purpose worker who fit into any role as required. He may have started here as a ward boy, but his warm heart and keenness to learn had gradually earned him the respectable title of an all-rounder who could be relied upon to do whatever he was entrusted with. He had a smile on his face at all times and was always on the go.

Sudha Vahini (Haribhau's wife). She was, perhaps, a few years older than us, as was her husband. Hence the deferential suffix-Vahini- was attached to her name. She was never an employee of the hospital but she found work very easily. She was everyone's assistant. Moreover, we had employed her to manage our house. She cooked breakfast, lunch, evening tea and dinner. and she cooked well! She also did our washing, cleaning and grocery shopping if we didn't have time to do it ourselves. She ruled over us through our perpetually empty stomachs. We really couldn't do without her.

Mukne.- The watchman. Actually there were two watchmen at the hospital but the other guy evades my memory save the fact that he had the alcohol habit and, as a result, was absent most of the time or ineffective when on duty. Mukne was an enterprising and smart young man. He was a local lad and had a flair for style. His clothes were tailored to fit and he always endeavoured to look like a dashing and debonair hero. Mukne was the messenger for all patients that arrived at the hospital. He would announce to us that some patient had arrived, and having apprised us of his arrival, he would step back and observe the medical drama unfold.

There were some more support staff but we had little interaction with them.

This was the one large family that worked together in the shockingly primitive conditions that prevailed in that area. Yet a lot of good was done for a lot of people. We had our share of tragedies too.

The Hospital and the Work.

The Patangsha Cottage Hospital was a primary care surgical centre. It served the most peripheral humanity, people who could not come to the towns or cities for medical treatment. The medical officer posted here was usually a surgeon and was capable of taking care of the patients in the early stages of the disease. There would generally be two senior doctors, an anaesthetist, six interns and ancillary support staff. There were three wards, one for male patients, one for female patients and one maternity ward.

Every morning at 9, we would open the out-patient department (OPD) and see the patients that would visit the hospital for their various ailments. In most cases medications and some motivational advice would suffice but when things seemed bad, we would have to admit them to the hospital ward. There were days when things were bad and we would have a stream of admissions, often necessitating mattresses on the floor to increase accommodation in the ward. In the interest of efficiency, and to enable us to finish the work on time, some of us would work in the OPD and others would work in the wards. Generally two interns would be required in the OPD as there was always a rush of patients.

The work never ended. We just stopped when we were exhausted. On most of the days we were very busy with an occasional lull interspersed. I guess, as we got seasoned by the work, our efficiency increased and we were able to finish more in less time. We also learnt in time, who needed more attention and who could be pushed away. There was an interesting custom at the hospital and we soon realised what was happening.

Early in the game we had subdivided the patients into townspeople and the Adivasis. The townspeople were relatively well-to-do and the Adivasis were extremely poor. There was a stark difference in the culture, demeanour and habits of the two classes. As far as possible, we tried not to be differential in our behaviour and tried to treat each kind equally. However, human nature being what it is, we always favoured the adivasis because they were the underdogs. When they had no one to speak for them, we would speak for them. Soon we became immensely popular with them and they started coming to us from far and wide. We would have so many of them waiting patiently outside the clinic every morning, never pushing or rushing us. We would see all of them. They had so many problems!

Problems of health were related to social, economic, environmental, nutritional and so many other reasons. Their plight was so severe, yet they endured. They took endurance to unimaginable heights. That's the reason why we had a soft corner for them. They had hearts filled with love, and their compassion was inimitable. They cared for human life and for each other. They left no stone unturned to help their fellowmen and hence an Adivasi patient never ever came alone. There would be at least two if not ten in a group with the patient. This was their support system.

On one particular day the local politician sent his secretary to find out when he could see us. We chose not to answer and said that he would have to come and see the Medical Officer. We were too junior and too busy to see him. The secretary tried his best but we didn't relent. We had discussed this matter earlier and had decided that we would never see the townspeople out of turn. Whoever they may be. This was our youthful, self-righteous defiance which sometimes got us into trouble.

The news had spread that there were some new doctors from the city at the cottage hospital. The medical care being what it was, everyone was ready to try out a new doctor. The general belief was that doctors who came here for their internship were very good. In keeping with that belief, the local politician was trying to solicit an opinion. We, on the other hand, hated to treat the townspeople because they took us for granted, exploited us. Ostensibly, because we were fresh medical graduates and seemingly knew a lot of modern medicine, and had a good bedside manner, they would keep on and on asking questions and take up a lot of our time. So we had decided that the townspeople would be seen by the CMO or the AMO, and we would see the Adivasi patients.

At this point in time we did something we would never repeat in future......

One day a local townsperson came to the clinic and demanded to be seen immediately. He was rude and arrogant. He had this feeling of entitlement which stems from having a little more wealth than the others. Despite having access to private practitioners they chose to come to us because they got the best advice for free at our hospital. This gentleman was trying to force himself in and dominate over us, insisting that he be seen first. Exasperated by his behaviour, we decided to teach him a lesson....

We took him in and asked his history and all his symptoms. Thereafter, we gave him a strong dose of a laxative, and a small dose of a diuretic. This would not only cause him a lot of distress but would keep him busy for many hours, after which, we thought, he would never return to us. Indeed, it did have the desired effect and he had a very exuberant reaction entailing several urgent visits to the toilet which had him exhausted by night. The next day he complained to the CMO and we were all summoned. Whilst reprimanding us, even he couldn't help smiling at the infantile practical joke we had played on the hapless, arrogant patient. Needless to say, he never showed up at our clinic again!

Our work was busy and mainly comprised of patients suffering from dehydration due to diarrhoea, vomiting, or both. This was interspersed with the urgent call to attend to a delivery. Deliveries happened at any time and almost every day. We would admit the patients who were at full term and keep them under observation, watching the rate of uterine contractions and preparing for their deliveries. Most of the deliveries were done by the nurses, who were experienced midwives and ANMs (auxiliary nurse midwife). They had done scores of deliveries and, if at all our presence was required, it was only for our own learning process rather than the girls receiving some guidance from us. The rule book, however, specified that no delivery will be conducted without the attendance of a qualified medical practitioner. Well! We were thus given a share of the credit. In the bargain we were taught the finer nuances of managing a delivery.

In one month I was a veteran at managing a pregnancy. We used to run the ante-natal clinic which enabled the Adivasi women to have a thorough examination during pregnancy, and guidance and supervision during delivery. None of them ever needed surgical interventions under the caesarian section. They delivered normally, braving the pains as the most natural thing under the sun. They would scream and moan, but never once suggested an alternative to a normal delivery. Surgeries were rare at this hospital until one day........

10. Dhavali

It was a wet day in late September. Busy as usual, with so many cases of diarrhoea, vomiting, fever, and some other trivial complaints. Dadan and Motwani were with me. Just as we were about to get back to our quarters we got a call from the senior midwife and nurse saying that there was a pregnant woman at the doorstep of the hospital. We looked at each other, wondering who would take the call. We were all tired and had had enough for the day. Nevertheless, we decided to go to the ward to see who this new patient was.

There, on the ledge, sitting huddled in an old bed sheet, was this Adivasi girl. She was shivering from the cold and she was wet, weak and hugely pregnant. Whilst taking her history we realised that she had walked or been carried by her husband from a village very far away. My estimate could be about 60 km.. She was exhausted! On a closer look we realised that she had severe swelling on the legs right up to the thighs! She was dark-skinned, yet the skin had a pale look. Her conjunctiva was almost white.

One look at her eyes, and the helpless look on the husband's face and there was no doubt in our minds that we would have to admit her immediately. We brought her in and put her on a bed. The nurse promptly started drying her with a towel. After making her comfortable and putting a dry sheet over her to make her warm, we did the rest of the examination. The edema had caused a serious swelling in her vulval region and it was almost impossible to see the outlet of her vagina. There was some swelling on her abdomen too. The uterus was hard. It had been contracting from the previous evening.

It had taken them 24 hours to reach us as they had no transport. Dhavali, this Adivasi girl, had walked the distance with her husband, leaving their farm unattended, resting periodically and sometimes being carried.

It was way past sundown, the lights in the ward were bleak, and cast a pall of gloom in that ward. Dhavali was really sick, and we were in a dilemma as to what we could do next for her. We could have shifted her to Thane Civil Hospital but that was too far away for her to make it. She was poor, and she was without any means of going any further without posing an immediate risk to her life. We had to treat her here and now! We had no choice. If we didn't treat her, she was ready to die!

We drew blood for some urgent tests, a urinary catheter was installed so as to help her pass urine, and to help us know how much she was passing. We had to get a lot of water out of her body and.... fast! She was already in labour for more than 16-18 hours and the uterus was in full contraction presently.

The abdominal examination felt like there were limbs all over the place. "Hey! What's this? I can feel so many limbs. Have a look?" So saying, I invited the others to give their opinions. Hiroo looked. Dadan looked. Both were non-plussed.

"Really, it's difficult to say. The uterus is so tightly contracted."

There was no way we could tell what exactly we were feeling through the tight wall of the uterus. She was in labour, but was making no progress towards delivery. She was in agony, and something had to be done really fast. Whilst we were debating on what should be done, the nurse had collected blood and come back saying that the hemoglobin was only 5 gm%.

"Only 5gm%!" we exclaimed in unison. That was worrisome.

"Now what?" No time to think! No time to seek help! No time to delay!

The way Dhavali was progressing she looked like she would collapse any moment from sheer exhaustion and pain. She was in obstructed labour and something had to be done. We were all tired, hungry, and presently mortified. Here was a young girl, pregnant, malnourished, bordering on collapse due to exhaustion and in obstructed labour. Add abject poverty to the list and she had nowhere to go.

What should we do? That was the thought running through our minds.

"Let's cut her open!"

"Are you mad or what?"

"We have no choice! Either we try saving her by cutting her open or else....... Or else she will die whimpering in front of our eyes!"

"But.........?" Hiru paused, thinking....

"We never did a Caeser before."

"I have assisted in several. I know the steps."

"Nisal! He is a gynaecologist! He will do the surgery! We can help him."

Though he was a gynaecologist we had never seen him doing any surgery. His standard excuse was that the operation theatre was not upto the mark. Not equipped or not sterilised.... Any excuse to stall the surgery. Here was the golden chance to see how he responded.

"Start an intravenous drip for her, normal saline, keep it at 20 drops per minute. Give her a hot sponge bath, especially her abdomen and back,...... We are going to talk to Nisal upstairs." So saying, we turned to go.

The nurse, who was tending to Dhavali, suddenly exclaimed, Sir! "Her fetal heart sounds......!" Excitement was writ large on her face as she extended the fetoscope towards us, beckoning urgently to listen to them for ourselves. "The baby is alive!" She was wide-eyed in her excitement.

Dadan bent down to listen to the fetal heart sounds with the primitive fetoscope.

A fetoscope is a conical, aluminium instrument which, when abutted against the abdomen of the pregnant girl at a strategic point, could enable you to hear the fetal heart sounds when the ear was placed at the other end of the cone. More than hear, one could feel the sounds in the ear. It took a lot of practice and concentration to be able to hear the fetal heart sounds with this simple instrument.

Having spent so many nights at Cama Hospital in Bombay was actually paying rich dividends now. At that time, during our urban internship, we were loathe to stay and needed any excuse to 'bunk' ob-gyn emergency duties. "Who wants to be a gynaec anyway!" would be the common refrain amongst the boys who were always looking to shirk work. Then Korde Madam would issue a 'warrant' for those who were not present in the labour ward in the night and make them do additional duties. Reluctant though we were, we had attended all the duties and assisted in more than a hundred deliveries. Some may have been by forceps application, some by surgical intervention, but most were delivered normally. We had become adept in the art of encouraging a pregnant woman to push her baby out the normal way. We had learnt how to 'iron the vagina' to help it stretch, so that the baby's head could descend.

We also learnt the value of an episiotomy, an intentional incision to widen the birth canal, to prevent a jagged tear of the perineum due to a difficult delivery. Sometimes, when the baby's head is large or the baby is large, the perineum gives way and ruptures down the centre and thereafter the rent in the tissue doesn't heal as well as it should.

We had spent many an enjoyable night in the labour ward anteroom waiting for some action. Till the actual action took place, we became adept at providing our own action in the form of impromptu musicals, mimicry and midnight feasts, either from some classmates home or from some restaurant nearby. Drudgery and the waiting game had to be made endurable.

Meanwhile, Dadan, who was listening intently, suddenly exclaimed, "Arrey! There are two heart beats! I mean, two separate heart beats! Look!" he adjusted the fetoscope at the exact location where the sounds were best audible and beckoned, "See ! Here is the first and here is the other!" his voice was agog with excitement. "She has twins, re!"

"Wow! TWINS!!"

"She has twins!"

".......and both are alive!"

We HAVE to do something, yaar. Call Nisal ! Fast!!"

"Sister, get her cleaned up. Do as I told you. We are going and preparing for the surgery."

Hiroo, you go to the OT and check the instruments. I'm going to talk to Nisal. Dadan, you stabilise the patient....... We'll do the surgery."

11. Take her for Surgery!

We all hurried to our separate destinations.

Dadan to get the IV drip. Hiroo to fix the OT....... and I took the steps on the double to Dr. Nisal's home on the first floor.

I knocked on his door urgently. He opened the door tentatively. He had already changed into his night wear and was probably getting ready to sleep.

"What's the matter, Gokani?" he asked me.

Sir! .... We have an Adivasi .... girl in obstructed labour. 5 gms haemoglobin ...... Massive edema ..... exhausted....... and we think there are twins!" Spewing the history even as I was trying to catch my breath.

He stood dumbstruck at the door. Not believing what he had just heard. What I had just informed him could be any surgeon's nightmare. Very high risk, yet mandatory. Enough to put your mind out of gear in a jiffy, especially when the infrastructure was so deficient.

When did she come here?"

"Just came in, Sir. In the last half an hour."

"Transfer her to Thane Civil Hospital. We can't do such complicated cases here. Ask her husband to arrange an ambulance and take her there." So saying, he was about to shut the door.

"Sir, they are very poor. Sir, they have walked for almost 20 hours to get here despite the rain. We can't send them away in this state. Sir, she will die for sure if we don't help her. She is exhausted!" I was almost pleading with him to let us do the surgery.

"We can't do this kind of surgery here," he said matter-of-factly.

"Sir,......please. listen to me, sir. She has obstructed labour. She is not progressing. Her Hb is low, too low. She is exhausted. And she has twins that are alive! ....

Sir, if we operate on her we can save three lives. Sir, we will help you. Hiru is good at surgery.... and I have seen a lot of Obgyn work.

Sir, let's give it a shot! Nothing to lose....... nothing at all."

Nisal was listening. He was thinking. He was absorbing this tirade at his doorstep, late at night. He saw the earnestness on the young intern's face and suddenly changed his stance. "Okay. I'm coming down in five minutes. Let me change my clothes."

"Okay, Sir."

I ran down the stairs to tell everyone that Nisal had agreed. Hiroo was still rummaging in the OT, along with the OT assistant and Haribhau, trying to get the instruments that we would be needing. Dadan had got the patient cleaned up and the drip was flowing.

There was no letting up in the contractions. Now they were almost continuous.

We reassured the distraught and defeated young husband. He was tired, from his long trek in the rain, and now, with the prospect of losing his wife from childbirth. Just looking at him, huddled in the corner on the floor, shivering in the wet clothes and burying his head in the palms of his hands,... one couldn't tell whether he was shivering or sobbing. or both.

I got a blanket and draped it on his shoulders so that he could wrap himself in it. I asked Vahini to get him something to eat. There was our dinner in the quarters, the dinner which we had not been able to have. I asked her to give him some from there.

Nisal arrived in ten minutes. Examined Dhavali. He realised that she was sinking. No time to reach Thana Civil! It was do or die. So he decided.... DO!

"Where is Hiroo?"

"In the OT."

"Okay."

"Take her in and change her into the OT clothes. What about the anaesthesia? Ujwala is on leave."

"Sir, spinal. I'll give. I've done it before."

"We can't do that. I'm not going to operate unless we have an anaesthetist."

"But..... Sir,.... She will die if we don't. We have to give her a chance."

"Sir. Come on, Sir!"

"The OT is ready, Sir. Come on, Sir, we don't have any option."

We were persistently and vehemently egging him on. If he didn't operate we wouldn't be able to do anything. We needed him to cover up for us if things didn't work out. We were all charged up and ready to go ahead. No rest, no food, tired from a tough day, yet rearing to go. To save her life. And maybe her twins. The thought itself was so exciting.

12. Surgery!

Dhavali was wheeled into the OT at about 11 at night. She had had nothing to eat for so long, hence the risk of vomiting owing to anaesthesia was minimal. And, anyway, our main aim was to give her the best chance to get out of this mess she was in, hence we didn't have any choice. Her pains were becoming unbearable for us to witness. Her screams were less powerful, her energy was ebbing.

Dhavali, the name derives from the word, white. It was ironic that she would have a name which meant white, whereas actually she was so dark. The whites of her eyes and her uneven yet beautiful teeth were the only whites on her. She lay there on the operation table, listless, weak, and helpless. Swelling, pallor marring her countenance. Her hair was bedraggled from her long and arduous journey through rough terrain and heavy rain, and face, tear- stained and contorted in fear and pain. She was wailing in agony, begging for relief.

We had a quick word with her and tried to reassure her. We needed her fullest cooperation, at least what she could give us. It was a moment of trial.

The OT was a small room. Not air-conditioned! No chance!

Haribhau in the flanks, waiting for the odd job that may be required. The veteran Maushi, the midwife, for assisting in the care of the babies when they were brought out. Dr. A. B. Nisal, the Obstetrician-in-chief at present, Dr. Dadan, the acting Paediatrician, Dr. Hiroo Motwani, the Surgeon, and Dr. Anand Gokani, the acting Anaesthetist and Assistant Surgeon. The OT assistant was there too. The team was ready. The patient was ready. The big moment had arrived.

Exactly three hours ago, we had called it a day and were ready to get to our room for a simple dinner, and some fun amongst ourselves, to unwind after a particularly tiring day. And here we were. Far from fun and games, far from food and water, fatigue and hunger forgotten, ready to play God for a helpless girl, hovering on the brink of total collapse.

"How would you like to give the anaesthesia?"

"Sitting."

"Okay."

"Mama, make her sit up and hold her in position." She was helped up to a sitting position and made to crouch such that the spine took the shape of a C. However, as soon as we saw the way she was crumbling in the sitting position we put her back on the table. Suddenly a sense of severe apprehension crept in on me.

Are we doing the right thing?

What if she died on the table.....because of what I had done...... or because of something that may go wrong?

What if she collapsed while giving her the spinal injection? Her husband would think that she was killed by us. One moment she is alive and wailing, in pain, in agony....... And in the next moment she collapses and dies.

How will we be able to explain all this to the distraught husband?

A shudder of self doubt ran through my body.

Was I a maverick who had conned everybody into believing that we could pull this off?

Should we still step back and give her up?

Something inside me said,"You're her only hope. It is actually a 'do or die' situation."

So this time, amidst all my self doubt and confusion, I had to convince myself that there was no choice but to DO!

After laying her back on the table we turned her to her left side and tried to arch the spine in the most gentle manner possible under the circumstances. A vision of all the lumbar punctures I had done during my urban posting, flashed through my mind. It was like an express train that ran through my mind in a fleeting vision. Every step of the procedure was visualised in a second....... from a pre-existing bank of experience.

We painted the lower spinal area with spirit first, then an iodine solution and then spirit again. Back then, betadine was not there in the market, so obviously, one had never seen it in the village. After due asepsis, the area was draped and the spinal space identified.

Edema had blurred the landmarks and the pregnant state made ideal positioning well-nigh impossible. The long spinal needle was gently inserted after giving a spot of local anaesthesia. It went in easily. Forwards and upwards towards the umbilicus from the back. There was a 'give' as the spinal needle pierced the meninges.

Gently, ever so gently the needle was pushed into the spinal canal. The trocar was then removed, with bated breath.

Am I in the right space or not?

Will there be a signal flow of spinal fluid?

What if nothing comes out? .... Or worse still.... What if there is bleeding? I'd have botched it up right at the start.

Trepidations.... Anxiety!

Everyone was watching anxiously as I pulled the trocar out. And as it came out.... out came the spinal fluid, clear and untarnished by blood. There was a restrained yelp of joy. That's nice! First step done!

The next step was to push the xylocaine into the spinal canal through this needle. I'm not mentioning the dose because, in all honesty, no one knew exactly how much to put, so we thought we would play it by ear. We put about 3ccs and waited. After a minute we asked her to move her legs. She was unable to move them and she was unable to feel any sensation below the umbilicus.

"Okay, Sir. Okay, Hiroo.You can start."

Hiru put the first incision. It was not the Pfannenstiel incision, as is used in the major centres, where experienced doctors do the surgery. This was a para-midline incision just below the umbilicus till the lower end of the abdomen. This is the safe incision. Having made the incision through all the layers of the abdomen, they reached the uterus which was there in all its majesty, now in full view. Owing to the anaesthesia the uterus had relaxed. The incision was widened to accommodate the uterus and, when the uterus was fully visible, we had the next dilemma.

"Sir. I can't do the lower segment incision. I don't know how to save the uterine arteries."

"I don't feel comfortable doing the lower segment incision without back up either. I wouldn't risk it to bring the kids out. A nick on the uterine artery would be lethal on the spot. The uterines are very tortuous in pregnancy and so full of blood."

"Then? What should we do?"

"Do the classical, from the top of the uterus. That's the safest bet."

"We'll do the classic fundal incision." Having said this, Dr. Nisal made the incision right across the top of the body of the uterus. In a moment there was a gush of amniotic fluid. The assistant was ready with the suction machine and, within moments, he had the nozzle pointed at the fluid and all of it was travelling down the suction catheter. Yellowish green in colour.

"The liquor is meconium stained!"

FETAL DISTRESS!!"

13. Triumph and Happiness!

That was a call for emergent action. The momentary elation of having successfully reached this level of surgery was replaced by anxiety again. We didn't want to lose what we had so painstakingly preserved thus far.

The foetuses were in distress as evidenced by the green meconium in the liquor, which is, otherwise, straw coloured. Meconium is the very first stool of a new born and is passed after birth. If it is passed before delivery it stains the liquor or amniotic fluid green.

"Dadan! Maushi! Get ready!"

One hand inside the uterus, Dr. Nisal hooked a finger around a dainty-looking arm and pulled it out, soon to be followed by the shoulder, then the head and then the entire body. The first baby was out.

Dadan received the puny little bundle of life. A tiny yelp was followed by several feeble cries. The baby was alive and breathing. The OT was a picture of fleeting ecstasy for a moment before the hand plunged in for the second one.

Within moments there was a second yelping bundle of joy coming out of her abdomen. Maushi had taken custody of the first baby. And was wrapping it in cotton wool and then in a sterile green cloth. The second was similarly wrapped. Both the infants were small and light, but they were crying and the breathing looked normal.

Dr. Nisal was triumphant and elated with the success. He was beaming, circumspect and smug with the success so far.

"Closure. Hiroo? Shall we close now."

"Yes Sir."

14. Post Op

Looking towards the OT assistant, Hiroo said, "Pass me the catgut."

"Here, Sir."

"This looks too thick." Hiroo looked at the material in his hand quizzically.

"That's all i can find."

"Okay." Hiru and Dr. Nisal started suturing the uterus. Within the next fifteen minutes the uterus had been secured by the 'catgut'.

"Motwani, will you close the abdomen?"

"Yes, Sir?"

"I'll go now. Good job boys. Gokani, your anaesthesia lasted for the entire surgery. Very good. I didn't realise that you guys are so good." He was visibly delighted with the job done so far. Looking to the OT assistant he said,"Arrey, show me the catgut packet we used. I don't remember ordering such a thick variety. When did this come?" The assistant rummaged in the refuse bin and came up with the packing of the suture material used.

Hiroo was suturing the abdominal wall, Dadan and Maushi were fussing over the babies who had settled down now. I was temporarily redundant as the work was almost done, i sat on the stool looking on at the last phase of the drama that had unfolded over the past three hours. Dr. Nisal received the remnants of the packet from the assistant. One look at it and his face blanched and then, slowly, he turned red!

"What did you give me, you fool!? This is Shirodkar's suture for the cervix! And I used it to close the uterus! It is NOT catgut! Who made you an assistant? Mad.......?" Nisal was livid. Having let loose on the OT assistant he stormed out of the OT muttering profanities under his breath.

There was an uneasy silence in the OT. Thus far, everything had gone well and, considering the circumstances, we had done well for ourselves and for Dhavali. Now, all of a sudden, not all is well. Now what? Everyone was silent as Hiroo continued to tie the sutures to the abdomen, deep in thought.

"Hiroo, the anaesthesia is wearing off. I think she feels the pain. Close soon. Forget the wrong material. We will deal with it after building her up a bit. For the time being let's not sweat this error!"

"Okay, last suture. I can't still believe that we did all this. Really, with nothing here we did so much. Hope all goes well." There was a sense of fulfilment and an anticipation of what the morrow had in store for us. This was just the beginning.

15. Our Next Dilemma

Dhavali was wheeled out of the OT on a trolley and taken to the maternity ward. The maternity ward was nothing like the sophistication of modern hospital wards. It was a shed with beds lined up across its length. She was given a bed near the door, more by coincidence than by design. The babies were placed next to her. After washing up from the surgery, it was now time to examine the babies. They were six on the APGAR score and cause for concern. The focus of anxiety was inexorably shifting from the mother to the babies.

No sooner we shifted Dhavali to the wards, and her anaesthesia started wearing off, she started moaning and squirming in pain. The only pain killer we had was analgin. To give or not to give? Another dilemma. Analgin had the strong propensity to cause bleeding in the stomach, and with her low levels already, we couldn't risk her bleeding even a drop from anywhere.

Fatigue had again raised its head and hunger clawed our insides. Dinner had gone to someone more needy and so we had next to nothing in our room. Yes! There were some biscuits. They could assuage our hunger for a while. As Vahini had retired for the night our next meal would hopefully be only at breakfast.

Turning our attention to the babies once again, one of us remarked, "What about breast milk? Don't we have to give the babies some feed.?"

Just then, Maushi dropped a bombshell. Dhavali had not a drop of milk in her breasts. She was dry! With such a low haemoglobin and protein levels in her body she was unlikely to be able to make milk for her babies. That was the last straw on the proverbial camel's back. "Ata kay? Now what?" That was a question on everyone's mind. None of us had the experience of handling premature babies, especially enfeebled, underweight, newborn twins! The double delight quickly changed to double anxiety. Now what!

"Can we give Cerelac?" without a thought I asked this question. A typically city-bred elitist question.

"Anand....... You're not in Bombay! Here they don't know what is Cerelac. Never heard of it. And ...mila bhi toh.......Who will pay for it?

"Now we were treading on the darkest of dark areas. Hitherto, we all had had some experience during our urban training in Bombay at JJHospital, under the guidance of super-specialists. This, however, was going to be our nemesis. What to do was the next dilemma. After some discussion we agreed to give the babies plain distilled water until the next morning and then take it as it comes. Dhavali was stable, her Haemoglobin had dropped to 3 gm% and she was weak and restless. The cause of her problem, however, had been dealt with and the joys of motherhood overtook the pain, the agony, the terror, and the uncertainty of the future. She was so much better than she was a few hours ago. Her vitals were okay and she was stable.

We advised three bottles of fluid overnight till the end of the next day and injectable Streptopenicillin every twelve hours. Streptopenicillin was a combination of streptomycin and penicillin and was the only antibiotic available to us for any disease. If the patient could afford it we would prescribe injection ampicillin which was a new antibiotic and very expensive.

We asked the nurse to watch her carefully overnight. To watch for bleeding, abdominal distension, fever, a drop in her blood pressure and/ or any change in her breathing. There were no intestinal sounds audible yet, hence we didn't advise any food or water for her.

We were exhausted, hungry and sleep deprived. It was 3am by the time we had settled the patient. We dispersed to have a cursory look at the other patients in the ward, just to ensure they were stable, so that we wouldn't have to come back before the morning.

There was a sense of fulfilment..contentment,...a kind of joy that supervenes at the end of it all. The fatigue and hunger seemed unimportant in comparison. As we made our way back to the room, there was a silence and a stillness in the air, the kind that precedes the dawn of a new day. No one had the energy to wash up. We just crept into bed and slept, oblivious of the world around us or the hunger and fatigue within. Vahini would make us breakfast in the morning.

16. The Twins

The next few days promised to be as harrowing and tense as the day gone by. The twins looked too small. They were far too feeble and we didn't have the sophistication, available to us in a city hospital, to manage them well. Most importantly, we didn't have a source of food for the kids! Overnight, the kids had been given distilled water but now we had to give them milk. After some deliberation we arrived at a concensus solution of giving them half diluted cow's milk.

We had a daily supply of cow's milk from a local farmer who we had treated in the past. This was used to make tea for us twice a day. About half a litre was what we had. We sent word to the farmer that we needed more as we had this new crisis to deal with. He said that he had already committed his supply and had no surplus as his cow gave a fixed amount of milk every day. However, he promised to do his best. If at all, it would only be available from the next day. So, for that day, we used the milk that we had. We needed a quarter of a litre of milk to feed the kids and we had that amount.

The first feed of diluted milk was given at 8am, given carefully with a dropper, by the most experienced nurse in the hospital. The kids had 30 ml of this formulation each and there didn't seem any problem. We were very happy. The next feed was scheduled for 10am.

We hurried through our rounds and daily routine, still hungover from the excitement of the previous night's happenings. We were filled with the anticipation of the events that would follow in the course of time. The questions coming up in our minds were. Will the kids survive?...Will Dhavali survive?...What if.......? A thousand questions arose in our minds but.... The answers? Only time would tell.

Dhavali was doing better. Her limbs were moving. The swelling already seemed to have regressed, and her vital signs were all stable. She could get off the bed and sit up. She was keen to hold her babies but we didn't want her to stress so we didn't allow her to handle them as yet. She was struggling with a million emotions. Joy, pain, weakness, anticipation, gratitude, relief and so many more. Her ordeal had ended. At least for the time being.

17. Careless!

The kids were tolerating their feeds so far. It was good going as the day wore on. The others in the ward were also stable. We looked forward to a good night's rest. Before we retired for the day we thought we'd look up the kids. The second born was so very small, just about the size of my palm. The first born was a bit larger. They looked so cute in the wraps, albeit cotton wool and cotton hospital sheets of cloth. There was a hint of redness on their faces. They were like miniaturised adults, or almost. We decided to give only water at night as the milk was over and the new stock would come only in the morning. We left the vials of distilled water with the nurse on duty and retreated to our rooms for the night.

A clean-up, a relaxed dinner and sleep. That's all we needed at this moment. We slept through the night.

There was frantic knocking on the door at about 6 am which shook us out of our sleep. At the door was the watchman, Mukne. He spoke in a frenzied tone, "Sir!, Sir!! Come soon. Something has happened to one of the kids."

"Coming!" I returned with him to the maternity ward where the kids had been kept with the mother. Everyone was standing there, aghast! The smaller kid was in Maushi's hands and she was looking distraught. I took the child from her hand. He was pale, and lifeless.... I gently put him down on the bed and examined his chest.There were no breath sounds. There was no heart beat. There was no effort to take a breath.The child was dead!

"What happened?" I asked Maushi. She was on the verge of tears. She knew how hard we had worked to save the kids. How much we had all wanted to get the kids some nourishment. She was disappointed too. Beyond words. She didn't say anything. The tears just kept pouring down her cheeks, misting her thick glasses.

Dhavali was also crying silently. Her little cup of joy already seemed to have emptied by half. I placed the infant on the bed, called for a white sheet of cloth, draped him in the cloth and handed it over to Dhavali's husband. As the impact of his child's death hit him he broke down, hugging the little bundle close to his chest. His shoulders shook with the silent sobs. I placed my hand on his shoulder and just stood there silently conveying my feelings to him. He soon pulled himself together. He later left the hospital to bury his son. For long after he left, there was a silence in the room. As though time had frozen every breath.

I turned my attention to the other child. He looked quite well so far and holding on, oblivious of his brother's death. I took Maushi out of the room and asked her, "What happened?"

She said, "The night girl ran out of distilled water and so she gave the infant some of the ward water. In the morning, the infant had two large loose motions and then....," Maushi started sobbing again, ".......and then the child just became limp and collapsed. The water was not right for the child."

She knew, and I understood, what had transpired. The infant was, indeed, too fragile to be able to fight any source of infection. The enormity of our problem was all the more evident to us after this loss. Saving the babies was not dependent on one thing, one factor or one person. Innumerable factors would have to be contended with, if we were to give this second one a fighting chance. Nothing in this hospital would change in a hurry and, given the resources, the environment and the level of experience, saving the second one was going to be a superhuman task. We were up against too many odds.

Why did the night girl give the ward water to the baby?...

Why didn't she ask us?...

She could have sent a call and we would have attended to the child.

Why...? Why...? Why...? So many questions. No answers.

In her infinite simplicity the girl didn't even realise that distilled water is so different from the water we drink. She presumed that, if one is over, the other would do. She just wanted to give the child water as she thought it was thirsty. Just an act of kindness and of love. She never imagined, that this child could be so fragile, as to not be able to handle simple drinking water.

The child's death was weighing heavy on everyone's mind. A pall of gloom hung over the hospital. The staff here had seen many an emergency in their careers but rarely did they get to be part of such a dramatic case. Dhavali's case had, in some way or the other, involved everyone in the hospital. Hence Dhavali's loss was shared by everyone to the fullest.

The rigours of rural practice, the joys and disappointments of working with frugal means, the vagaries of human apathy, ignorance and illiteracy, so starkly accost you at such times. The feeling of total helplessness overpowers you. That was exactly what was happening to me.... and I knew it was happening to my colleagues and all the hospital staff.

18. Tragedy Revisited!

The rest of the day was unremarkable. We left Dhavali and her husband to tackle their grief privately. The other infant was stable. The feed programme was all set and the supply of milk had been established. We had to plan Dhavali's food too, as she was now able to eat, as the effect of surgical stress on her intestines had subsided. We obtained some fruit from the market for her and were toying with the idea of getting her a protein supplement which she could take along with some milk. She would continue to have her normal food too. Her appetite was still poor, possibly owing to fatigue, grief, stress, and post-partum depression. Any, or all these factors, could be at play. We needed to come to terms with our own feelings.

Hiroo was going to deal with her dressings and was presently satisfied that there was no infection. With her low haemoglobin and proteins, and with so much malnourishment, she was really prone to an infection which could be life-threatening. Her protein deficiency was going to prevent wound healing hence Dhavali's nutrition was already a matter for serious concern.

The next two days were uneventful, both Dhavali and her son were holding out well. Dhavali had started eating better and she looked more cheerful. Rice, dal, vegetables, groundnuts, roasted grams, chapatis and milk were her staple foods. She was regaining her colour ever so slowly, yet surely. The baby was still a major cause for concern. We were unable to get his food formula right. The dropper-administered milk was not right. We had to sterilise the water, the milk, the dropper and the person administering the feed had to be very clean too. This was next to impossible in the village where sterility was not a well understood concept. It was impossible for the local people to comprehend the concept of sterility and, it wasn't possible for us to supervise every feed. We had tried in our limited way, and had tried really hard, but yet, a stone had been left unturned.

It was now six days since the fateful night when the twins were born, and three days since the younger one had passed away. Somewhere deep inside us we were beginning to feel that this child would make it, and we would be able to help it survive. He was a joy to behold. Though we didn't allow too many to handle this child, enough people came to the wards just to be able to hold the child for a brief moment, fondle and caress him or to say a word of encouragement to Dhavali. Despite trying to keep people away and to maintain a level of sanitation it was impossible to maintain that high level of cleanliness necessary for the situation.

We were dismayed, on the seventh day, to see the baby listless. The cry was feeble and the respiratory rate was high. Was he going in for infection? Lungs? We hardly knew how to look after a premature baby and now we had an infected baby on our hands. I called the others and apprised them of our latest predicament.

Everybody was dismayed. There was an air of apprehension and anxiety, almost bordering on despair.

We started him on a very small dose of ampicillin which was way beyond Dhavali's limited means. We had all chipped in and paid for it. It had to be procured from the local chemist and was quite expensive. With immense trepidation, we administered the drug. A look at the very small hands, feet and the small facial features was constantly reminding us of the fact that we were sadly ill-equipped to treat this little one properly. We were in an area of near total darkness as far as the child's management was concerned. Every dose went in with a fervent prayer, and we were hoping against hope, to see that child comfortable and well again.

The eighth day, dark and gloomy, didn't bring glad tidings at all. We were all having breakfast in utter silence, in deep thought and, it took no guessing, to know what was going on in every mind. We were wondering who would take rounds and who would go to the OPD. There was a secret dread in all our hearts, of what awaited us in the maternity ward and none of us really wanted to be the one in charge of that ward presently. We all knew that Dhavali's son was going to be precarious today. The frustration and concern compelled us to keep thinking of him, and the fear of being the one to preside over his deterioration, and to be left watching helplessly, was holding us back from going to that ward.

There are times in a doctor's life when he doesn't have the courage to face the patient, knowing full well that the patient needs him close at that time, more than ever before. Yet that turmoil prevents him from taking a step in that direction to grasp and control the situation. More so when the patient has reached that point of no return or the means of the treatment are not available. In this baby's case, the knowledge that we were utterly and comprehensively helpless in the management of this baby and that we had no options but to reassure and keep reassuring the distraught mother that we were doing our best, and that she should be courageous and stay as calm as possible, frustrated us endlessly. The first baby's loss was traumatic enough. This baby's loss would be a complete washout of all our efforts on that night, a week ago.

Hiroo and I headed for the OPD and Dadan took up the ward work. He chose to start from the maternity ward. On examining Dhavali's son he observed that his skin had a deep yellow discolouration.

Normally new born babies have a mild yellowness to the skin in the first week of life, but this was a deeper yellow. Physiological jaundice happens when the infants fetal haemoglobin, which is high, breaks down to the adult haemoglobin after birth, which is lower than its fetal counterpart. This yellowness or jaundice subsides in a week and doesn't need active therapy. Dhavali's son had a deep jaundice possibly due to a septic focus. He was heading for septicaemia ...widespread infection in the entire body.

Dadan hurried to the OPD to tell us,"Arre! That bachchu is deep yellow! Jaundice ho gaya hai!"

"Oh, no!"

"Put him in the sunlight!"

Sunlight helps to reverse the jaundice of the newborn by hastening the metabolism of bilirubin. "Hell! There is no sunlight.!" Outside, the sky was dark with rain clouds and not a sign of the sun.

"Shall we try phenobarb?"

"Why phenobarb?"

"I read it in Goodman-Gilman (the textbook of pharmacology) that phenobarb induces enzymes in the liver which metabolise the bilirubin rapidly so jaundice settles faster."

"Bloody nerd! You actually read that book. I skipped that chapter."

Despite the situation, I couldn't help smile.

"But where will we get it from?"

Phenobarbitone is a powerful barbiturate and hence not available in the open market. Only the big chemists were authorised to dispense this drug. We had to locate this drug at any cost!

"Let's ask Vashani to get it for us." Vashani, the pharmacist, was a man afflicted by intractable inertia. Never went out of his way to do anything remotely digressing from the routine, mundane acts. We had to energise him to get us this drug. We rose in unison to head for his room. As expected, he didn't have the drug, and it would take him three days to get the medication from Thane. This was a losing battle.

Dejected, defeated, Dadan made his way back to the wards to attend to the child and other patients. Dhavali was soothing the agitated child and was trying to give him the comfort that only a mother can. Dadan again took the child from the mother's arms and examined his chest. There were crepitations, crackling sounds on both sides of the chest and the child was gasping for breath. "Sister, how much ampicillin have you given to this child? Get the oxygen with the finest tubing you have and also get me an ampoule of wysolone."

The nurse arrived with the medication ordered. Dadan said to her,"Give him 2mg of wysolone subcutaneous, under the skin, on the abdomen, stat!" The sister rushed to comply with this order, knowing that wysolone, a steroid, was the last ditch effort to save the child. But alas! It was too little, too late! It didn't seem to have any effect. The gasping continued and the lungs seemed to be flooding with secretions. Dadan again made his way to the OPD to discuss further treatment. We were all at a loss. We had tried steam, decongestants, antibiotics, steroids, oxygen and a dose of bronchodilator drugs. Nothing seemed to make any difference?

Fatigue seemed to be getting the better of us. We could think of nothing, neither conventional nor out-of-the-box, to help this infant. The baby was refusing feeds completely and was breathless and yellow. The urine output also had diminished to a fraction of the original. We called Dhavali and her husband aside and explained the grave prognosis to them. It was, indeed, difficult to break this untoward news to them.

What can one say in such circumstances?

....Tell her that her second child was dying?

.... That we were helpless in the face of imminent disaster?

---- that we were at a complete loss and had very little left to offer?

Finally, we broke the news to Dhavali's husband. We had to inform him that his second baby, too, was dying. With a lump in the throat we spelt it out to him. He was inconsolable and kept pleading with his eyes to save the boy. That look of a father being bereaved, not once, but twice, in the same week, was a sight you don't want to see again. Never again! It shakes the heart-strings violently.

The baby struggled as the evening wore on. We had tried every trick up our sleeve and now were resigned to our dismal fate. The rest of the ward was quiet, as though in deference to the events that would make this the blackest of black nights.

At night, the child was slightly stable and it appeared that the respiration was less laboured. A glimmer of hope? We felt good momentarily and headed for dinner on a slightly more upbeat mood. A simple dinner of rice and dal, with chopped cucumber on the side, and a dash of lemon pickle, was our princely meal tonight. The meal was eaten in silence, more from fatigue than anything else. Apprehension lurked at the back of every mind and delved the silence of the night for an answer to our latest dilemma. How to save the little one!?

Things were still quiet after dinner so we decided to sleep. We tried....but sleep eluded us. We lay in bed ruminating. Thinking. Despite our fatigue there was no let up.

At 4 am there was a rap on the door, "DOCTOR! Sister wants you urgently!" Our hearts sank. Who would answer that call? I got up to go.

Dadan said," Do you want me to come? I'll come, if you want help."

"I'll call if i need help."

I reached the ward in half a minute. Sister was holding the baby between the palms and desperately pumping his chest with her thumbs. There was a deathly cyanosis on the baby's face, a deep shade of blue, and there was no spontaneous effort to breathe. I asked the nurse to hand me the child. She was distraught and desperate. Her face contorted with anxiety and fear. I took the infant gently from her hands and felt his chest for a heart beat. There was none. The child lay motionless in my palms. That perfect little baby, the little gentleman, he lay there at peace with himself and the world, oblivious of the feelings of the people around him. Oblivious of his parents' broken hearts, of the nurses' dismay, of his doctors' helplessness. He was gone, gone for good.

19. Grief!

I looked at Dhavali, who was staring at me with unseeing eyes. Dumbstruck! Benumbed! At a complete loss for words! Bereft of emotions! Overwhelmed!

The knot in my throat tightened as I gathered the courage to actually spell it out to them. She was just staring at the baby, lifeless, motionless, in my palms. Her husband, who was sleeping under the bed, awoke instinctively, as if sensing that something was gravely wrong.

The nurse came over to me, took the baby from my hands and proceeded to wrap him up in a white cloth. I put a hand on Dhavali's shoulder. This shook her out of her reverie and I saw the first tears leave the portals of her glazed and tired eyes. And then the dam burst...and she started sobbing uncontrollably. Her grief was indescribable. Her husband stood speechless and I could say nothing to them. I just stood there, transfixed. My hand on her shoulder racked by her sobbing. A sense of complete helplessness seizing me.

Apart from the unbridled grief, there was an eerie silence in the room. No one had any courage to speak. Nobody knew what to say. Just the lump in the throat that kept getting worse and something seemed to well up from inside. Men don't cry ...... I said to myself. I abruptly turned around and, giving the nurse a 'please take care of them' kind of look, I headed for the privacy of the nurses' station to make the papers......and deal with my feelings.

The night was restless. There was an unresolved grief within my heart and mind. A feeling of being let down. ....

..... By Fate .

..... By Nature.

..... By Circumstances!

It was the unacceptable ignominy of failure. We had failed the poor girl owing to inadequate experience, knowledge, support. We could not give her the gift of a child. We couldn't give her the benefits of modern medicine. We would never be able to reverse the events of the week gone by. This was a loss which would take years to recover from. The parents grief was palpable and there was nothing I could say or do to assuage their feelings.

Fate had no business to be so selectively unkind!!

Why!?.....

Why was God so unjust?!......

Why did the kids die so early?.....

What was the sin that was being punished?,...... And who committed it?

The parents? .....the kids? What kind of account was this that was being settled?

A million such questions tormented my mind. Sleep was a faraway thing. Knowing that there was a poor girl and her husband nursing a profound hurt, the hurt of a loss so grave, so immeasurably deep, kept hurting me from within.

Scarcely had her surgical wound healed, and her kids were gone.

20. Moving On

At the hint of daybreak, I decided to go out for a while. It was a cool morning, a nip in the air, a hint of light on the far horizon, clouds shrouding the imminent sunshine. The smell of wet earth pervaded the atmosphere. It was a new morning.

I slipped into my shorts and sneakers, and put on a tee-shirt and decided to take a walk. I needed to push the cobwebs from my mind and pull myself together. I had to go back to work and help the patients get better. I'd have to put yesterday where it belonged. ...... yesterday!

There was a road behind the hospital which was desolate. One rarely saw a vehicle on that road. I stepped onto that road feeling a sense of exhilaration. Soon the walk broke into a jog and my brisk steps covered the better part of a mile whereupon there was a diversion to the left. I followed the diverging track. Through the foliage and underbrush I walked on, and, before long, I was at a clearing. There, in front of me, was the glass-like surface of a lake.

This was the first time I had come upon this lake. I had heard of the dam being a scenic picnic spot from my colleagues but I had never imagined that I would come upon this lake so spontaneously and so suddenly. I thought it would be a planned trip someday.

The stillness of the lake was enchanting, captivating. I stood there, listening to the birds singing their daybreak melodies, the light breeze rustling the leaves of the trees. For long I stood before I moved over to the dam and found myself a place to sit and just bask in the soothing and calming effect of Nature. I could feel myself being rejuvenated.

The soft light of dawn, dulled by the cloudy sky, was slowly brightening the lakeside. This ambience had a healing effect on me and after spending half an hour by the lakeside I decided that I need to return and face the challenges of a new day. With the stresses of the week that was, placed firmly behind me, I started my walk back to the hospital.

The refreshing change from the hospital environment had already started me thinking of a new perspective to the same situation, a new dimension of all that had happened. Sometimes, it is not as we wish things to happen. It is not our wish that prevails, it is God's will that prevails. Much as we would like to disbelieve in such esoteric thinking, much as we would like to be rational and scientific, in the final analysis it boils down to God and his wish.

This is an unassailable fact that, sooner or later, will have to be accepted. What happens is not always what we want, what happens is always that which is good. There is always some hidden meaning in every little thing that happens and every event is created for our celestial education and experience. All we need to do is learn the lesson and move forward.

What had happened had happened. Now it was past. The only way now, was the way forward. So it was back to work with renewed energy. To make sure that all the patients got the best of my efforts. I just needed to learn that I must write these events in my book of experiences and to move on... A more experienced person.

The walk back to the hospital was exhilarating and refreshing. I thought I'd go to the wards for a quick look around before repairing to the room for breakfast. It was about half past seven and activities were just getting started. The patients were being given their breakfast and tea. A nurse was sorting the medications to be given to the patients. The patient I was seeking compulsively was Dhavali. She was on my mind and I needed to know that she was alright.

She was sitting up in bed, the lines of grief still etched on her face. Pain and anguish were omnipresent in her demeanour. Her husband was nowhere to be seen. He had probably gone to the cemetery to bury the second son. This thought itself re-awakened the anguish in my heart.

I stopped at Dhavali's bedside. She looked up to me, meeting my eyes with her eyes. I put my hand on her shoulder gently and asked her how she was. She just looked on, her eyes doing the talking, not a word escaping her lips. Her eyes said it all. She was grieved but she was going to be strong and she was going to get herself well. I waited with her for a long minute. Nothing was said but everything was implied and clearly understood. She dropped her gaze to rest on the cup of tea in her hand. Raising it, she took a sip, resolving to put the past behind her, and to embrace the moment and move on.

21. Theft

Over the next two weeks Dhavali made good progress. Soon after her surgery her wound had been filled with pus and she was running a light temperature. We had to start antibiotics again, adding to her weakness and slowing down her recovery. Gradually we overcame the infection. The secretions dried up, the haemoglobin rose to 7gms% and was rising steadily with the number of vitamins she was receiving.

Two weeks later, an emissary from Dhavali's village arrived, bearing more sad news. Whilst Dhavali and her husband were battling the greatest tragedy of their lives, somebody had stolen into their little farm and decamped with all the green chillies and vegetables which they had planted in order to sell and earn some money. Now they had nothing left. I learnt of this tragedy when I saw him sitting alone, near the entrance of the hospital, with anguish writ large on his face

I asked him,"What happened? Tell me?"

He said in a broken voice."My crops have been stolen!"

"Oh! I'm sorry! Now what will you do?"

"Doctor, I want to go home. I want to find out what happened and secure my home from other thefts. I can't leave Dhavali and I can't take her. If I leave her and go she will be upset. I don't know what to do......," and his voice trailed off, as he stared vacantly into space, searching for an answer to his new dilemma. "I need to be gone for at least four or five days it takes about one and a half days to reach home."

"One and a half days......?" I said this more to myself than to him, though I exclaimed aloud. I thought... it takes me 5 hours by bus to reach home about 160 km away...then why should he take one and a half days? "Why does it take so long? How far is your home from the hospital?" I was curious to know how far he needed to travel.

"If I go by bus, it takes one and a half hours, but I don't have the money to go by bus. I will have to walk the 60 km to my house, and that will take one and a half days."

I was painfully reminded of that night when he and Dhavali had walked from their home to the hospital in the rain and darkness. I reached out to him and told him to go and reassured him that we would take care of Dhavali. He looked at me, a bit non- plussed. I repeated what I said, "Tu ja ! You go! We will take good care of Dhavali."

Later that morning, when I told the others of this new development, about them losing their farm produce, we all felt and shared their grief. Hiroo, our finance manager, suggested that we give him the money required for the bus fare so that he can return soon. We all agreed. He prepared to leave the very next day.

22. Managing Money

Life at the hospital and in the village was simple. Very simple. Our needs were few and easy to satisfy. As interns we were paid a handsome stipend of Rs. 350/- per month by the government. As young, self-respecting doctors, we liked to live within our means and rarely asked our parents for supplemental expenses. In order to run our lives smoothly, whilst working here in the wilderness, we worked out a co-operative scheme.

Hiroo was appointed the 'finance minister' because he was meticulous in maintaining a note of the expenses. So it was decided that each one of us would contribute Rs. 300/- per month and share all the expenses. We had gone through the exercise of sitting across the table and calculating and formulating a budget for fruit, vegetables, kitchen ware, cooking gas, herbs and grains, other groceries, cleaning materials and salaries. If there was surplus money, then eggs and sweet meats could be indulged in.

The month started with a capital of Rs. 1800/- with which we bought stocks of wheat, rice, dals, sugar, vegetables, oil, salt, pepper, masala, tea, etc. and then allocated some for the purchase of fruit. Whoever was free, would visit the market to buy supplies, at least three times a week. As we had no refrigeration we had to buy stocks in just the right amounts, for a day or two. We could not afford losses due to spoilage. We also had a small salary for vahini and the maid who cleaned the house every two or three days.

If any money remained after making all the expenses mentioned above, then we were in for a treat. The treat being Rex Jelly! This was a treat without parallel. In addition we had so many sources of food which were spontaneous. For instance, when we treated an Adivasi and discharged him, often he would gift us with some produce from his farm. However small the gift, it meant the world for us because it came with so much love and respect. The Adivasi people were very quick to express gratitude and expressed it in a myriad different ways. Some were ongoing gifts, like the farmer who sent us half a litre of milk everyday, and there was at least one patient who would give us farm produce every day, and the gift would be like a rustic cucumber which was large, with large seeds and very sweet and refreshing when garnished with salt and red chilly powder. Sometimes we got green chillies, sometimes bananas, sometimes guavas.

Our life sustenance was thus well taken care of in this manner. The question arising maybe, "What became of the Rs. 50/- left after filling the kitty?" That money was to enable us to make a return trip to Bombay at a fare of Rs. 17.50/- per trip, rounding off to a return fare of Rs 35/-. Many times we didn't make that trip so we had the surplus money which was spent for buying antibiotics or other medications for the patients or paying for their bus fares or any other help that they may need. We lead a life of penury, but were very happy at the end of it. We survived on this shoestring budget for the entire tenure in the village, and returned, enriched with experience, wisdom, resilience, tenacity and so many other qualities and attributes that money cannot buy.

By standards prevailing in Jawhar, we were very wealthy and fortunate people. We had everything we needed. A roof on our heads and food on the table. We had clothes to wear, no ostentation, simple, clean and adequate clothes, at times slightly torn and repaired, but we never noticed these things, nor did we feel ashamed of being ill-clad. So many of our patients didn't have even this much. Yet, one never heard a whimper or complaint from them. If they couldn't afford something they would simply forgo it. They never asked for anything. Living amidst them, we learnt the value and meaning of simplicity. We always had so much more than them, despite our apparently extreme degree of thrift.

If at times our clothes were frayed, torn or not up to the mark, it didn't really matter because the people who we worked for, sometimes, didn't even have adequate clothes. The men would have a loin cloth and a sort of towel wrap-around and the women would be clad in half a sari. Living on a frugal budget taught us the real value of things we had in life, but took for granted. We appreciated, that living within our means meant to sacrifice somethings that we wanted, in preference for the things that we needed. We learnt to make do with less and less, and thereby focused on the things that mattered and the things that were priceless.

Our work and presence in the little town of Jawhar had, undoubtedly, helped so many people, who in turn, expressed there gratitude, not in cash but in kind. Their gifts enhanced our kitchen capabilities a great deal. The warmth and affection of the villagers made up for anything that we may have missed about city life.

Life here was hard, work was busy, but it was satisfying and rewarding in more ways than one. It was in these months that we learnt that there was much more to life than the mere acquisition of money, property and material wealth. Our slender finances helped us write another, unrecorded book of accounts. The kindnesses received from sources unknown, love received in doses unexpected and fulfilment received in magnitudes unimagined. Our physical penury was more than adequately compensated by the wealth of soulful experiences. Our pockets were empty but our souls were uplifted to heights beyond imagination.

23. Routine

Life at the cottage hospital had a kind of routine which was the baseline of activity. We had to wake up early. Vahini would arrive at 7.30 am to make us tea and some breakfast like sabudana (sago) vada or khichadi, upma or poha. Sometimes, if we were able to, we would go for a walk or jog, for a few miles down the road leading to Mokhada and be back for tea and breakfast. These mornings were the most beautiful ones, as we were in touch with raw, unadulterated Nature at its unspoilt best. The sunrise in Jawhar was the most beautiful in any climate. The chirping of birds, the sweet smell of wet earth, the subtle fragrance of some flowers mingled with the smell of cow dung lending the rustic charm to the ambience. There were no sounds of traffic, but for the rattling of wooden bullock carts, and the bells around the necks of cattle. The clip-clopping of hooves on the tar road would be the only vehicular sounds we heard for months. Cars were very rare, few and far between.

At 8.30 am we would start the outpatient clinic, where two interns would see all the patients reporting to the hospital with a wide variety of complaints. The other two would take ward rounds and would attend to emergencies. Hemant Painter really enjoyed the out-patient clinic. In order to enhance his credibility, he had invested in a headset attached with a mirror with a central hole, through which one could see the ear, the nose and the throat of the patient in more detail and in more clarity. We would frequently joke about his 'third eye' with which he could see things which none of us could. He was soon known by all as the doctor with the third eye.

The out-patient clinic was always packed and there was never a moment to digress from our work. These clinics saw patients suffering from coughs, colds, fevers, pneumonia, loose motions, constipation, pain in the abdomen, headaches, body aches, giddiness, vomiting, skin rashes, fractures or ulcers on the feet.....and so many other conditions that village people suffer from. Sanitation, boiling of water prior to consumption, cleaning vegetables before cooking them, ventilation in homes and personal hygiene were non-existent concepts to the village women. However, there were times when real emergencies would land up in our hospital. This would happen at least once a week.

24. Potya

One day a group of Adivasi men arrived at the clinic carrying a middle-aged man on a bed sheet as a makeshift stretcher. They had apparently walked many miles and the patient they carried was in a certain amount of distress. He was uneasy with pain and obviously very sick. He needed admission. He was seen in the clinic and immediately admitted. His main complaint was an acute pain in the abdomen with distension which had caused a lot of discomfort. enough to cause him some difficulty in breathing. He had been vomiting since three days and hadn't eaten anything since. He looked very dehydrated, his eyes were sunken, lips dry and chapped, the pulse was low in volume, with a rate of 120 beats per minute. The abdomen was tense and distended, there was a tympanitic sound on percussion, like there is when there is a lot of air in the intestine. The sounds of intestinal movements were absent. He looked like he had an intestinal obstruction with a resulting paralytic ileus. He needed advanced treatment. Most certainly surgical treatment.

Yogendra, Hiru and Dadan were seeing this case with me. We concurred that this patient needed to be urgently shifted to Thane Civil Hospital which was far better equipped to handle this emergency.

"Should we just hydrate this patient and send him to Thane?"

"I think that would be best. But....how will we send them? They have no means of transport. They have walked so many miles to reach here."

"That's a hugh problem."

"and the Thane ambulance is not due to come till Thursday. And it's only Monday. Don't think he will be able to wait till then."

"Do you think he can afford a private ambulance?"

One look at him and his family and their tired, helpless state didn't inspire the last possibility. There was no way they could reach Thane on their own steam. This was their destination, and having reached thus far, this was the end of the road for them.

"Let's talk to Dr. Nisal. We'll ask him if we can keep him here."

We started an intravenous normal saline drip and collected blood for a complete blood count, an ESR, and a sugar estimation. We also sent a sample of urine to the lab for analysis. It would have been nice to have an X-ray of the abdomen but the technician had been absent on health grounds since a while. Hence no X-rays were being done at the hospital.

Having started some supportive treatment we decided to talk to Dr Nisal. He was in his office. We entered and informed him the details of the case. He listened intently. After Dhavali's case he had a new and healthy respect for us and also a renewed interest in his work too. He knew that if he decided to undertake a tough case he had the support of interns to back him with sincere and dedicated aftercare. After we had apprised him of this case, he thought for a while, and then said, "Let's go and see him."

We returned to the patient's bedside together, and he examined him, like we had. The pulse was fast in rate but low in volume, the abdomen was tense and distended with mild diffuse tenderness. The liver and spleen were not felt. No lumps were discernible. The drip we had started was half done. We ordered for more, to be given rapidly, at the rate of one bottle over two hours, for the next three drips. We recorded the orders, emphasising that nothing should be given by mouth. Dr. Nisal suggested that we insert a Ryles' tube (a naso-gastric tube) to suck out the contents of the stomach and help in keeping it empty. Sometimes, this itself, is enough to help the patient to recover. One of us, immediately, got about the task of putting in the Ryle's tube. The procedure required us to get the written consent from the patient or his relatives allowing us to put the tube in. Taking a written and informed consent for any procedure was due diligence adopted as a good habit. Though the simple Adivasi folk didn't ever talk of litigation for things gone wrong.

Dadan had gone to the relatives to get the consent and he returned with a wry smile on his face, asking us, "Do you know his name?" We all looked non-plussed. In our concern for the patient we had not bothered to ask his name,"What's his name?"

"Potya!" Dadan said with a broad smile. "Potya!" He couldn't stop smiling despite the gravity of the situation. 'Potya' means 'related to the abdomen'. 'Pote' means abdomen in the local language.

How ironical. On hearing his name we couldn't help smiling broadly despite the prevailing mood of sobriety.

Yogendra was going to put the Ryle's tube and we were planning to observe Potya's progress for a while before making any further decisions. We still felt he needed a bigger hospital to get the best treatment, but there were just too many constraints. Potya was very sick. The friends and family were exhausted as they had trudged several miles to bring him to us, and they had no money to make the trip to Thane. Thane was a daunting city for these simple villagers. They were here to stay and we had to do whatever best we could.

Hydration with two drips afforded a marginal improvement. But there was no change in the abdomen. He had no appetite and was complaining of nausea. He had not passed any flatus, nor were there any bowel sounds. Intestinal paralysis! What could be the cause? This was the question on every mind. Could it be tuberculosis of the intestine? ...or Cancer?.....or....? The possibilities were all examined. The only thing discussed at lunch was this case.

This promised to be another rough case. Potya was in pain and was not getting better. He had exhausted his reserves and soon would start the downward spiral. We received his reports. The white cell count was 10,000/cmm and his haemoglobin was 9gm%. The urine report and the blood sugar were normal. We had no facility to do the electrolytes and other tests. There was absolutely no chance for an abdominal sonography report. We were well and truly constrained. The post lunch session was spent in observing Potya and noting his progress. The other patients were stable and no real cause for concern.

Dhavali, whose husband had gone to the village, was getting better too. She was less infected and she was eating better now. We had engaged her in trivial ward activities like rolling bandages and cutting gauze pieces which she happily did and that kept her mind occupied gainfully. She was still depressed but the love and kindness she received at the hands of the nurses, staff and doctors made up for her loss and kept her cheerful.

By tea time the abdominal girth had increased by a centimetre and things didn't seem right. What shall we do?

"I've started Streptopenicillin. Twice a day."

"Good."

"He needs surgery. Do you know anything about intestinal surgery?"

None of us had any first hand experience.

"If we don't do anything, he will die. If we operate we may lose him on the table.....or post op. Either way we are in a fix. They are not going anywhere else and have pinned their hopes on us."

"What shall we do?"

The shadows lengthened and dusk was fast approaching. The cows and buffaloes, hitherto grazing in the fields, were returning home. The rhythm of the bells, coupled with the hoof beats, pervaded the atmosphere at twilight. And....We were all stuck with a serious dilemma. Again it was the same. to do or not to do? And then. suddenly, there was courage from within. If we had to do something we should just do it. After getting my colleagues to concur, I proceeded to inform Drs. Nisal, Dhande and Ujwala. I informed them that the patient would need surgery. There was an initial objection from Dr. Nisal but after some discussion he realised the gravity of the situation and agreed to go along. Plans were made. Hiroo and Yogendra would assist Dr. Nisal. I would give the spinal anaesthesia again but this time Dr. Ujwala was there for moral support in case things didn't go right. Dadan was there too. In case of any other exigencies. The OT was made ready by the OT assistant and Haribhau. We planned on doing an exploratory laparotomy and were going to deal with whatever we found as best as we could. It was our only chance. Potya was wheeled into the OT at about 8.30 pm.

After duly checking all the lines and securing the Ryle's tube in place, we turned him to the left side and prepared his back for the lumbar puncture which would deliver the Xylocaine to the spinal canal. This was achieved without a flaw! The patient was turned on his back, the entire abdomen was first painted with spirit, then iodine and then spirit again. When we were sure the abdomen was clean Hiroo made the paramedian incision. First the skin, then the fascia and then the muscle.

"I've reached the inside of the abdomen. Should I free the intestine and bring it out?"

"Do that."

He extended the incision to the lower abdomen. The loops of intestine were visible now.

"Warm mops please. Keep them ready," he said, putting his hand into the abdominal cavity. "The loops are like balloons."He brought them out gently and Yogendra placed the warm mops on the intestine. About four feet of the intestines were brought out and were lying exposed on the operation table. They really looked distended. Dr. Nisal suggested that Hiroo feel the entire intestine along its length for a lump or any other abnormality. Putting his hand into the abdomen, Hiroo proceeded to feel the intestines and after a good five minutes of palpating he came out disappointed. "Nothing, Sir."

Looking over the shoulder I saw the loops lying there, outşide the abdominal cavity. Taking the intestine in his hands Yogendra said," Should we puncture the intestine and release the gas? He may be relieved." So saying, he pinched the intestine with a Babcock's forceps. As soon as he had done that the pinched part of the intestine turned black. There was a general gasp and in a chorus as it were, everyone said,"Take it off! Take it off !" He hurriedly removed the forceps, aghast with the result.

"If we puncture the intestine, none of us knows how to put it right. We don't have the materials or the know-how to repair a punctured intestine. In such circumstances it is best to do no harm," said Nisal. "Remove the mops and count them, replace the intestine and close as soon as you can. We'll see what happens later. If need be, we will transfer to Thane. I will make the arrangements,"

The mops were removed and counted, the intestines replaced and the abdomen closed, with the appropriate material, in layers. After Dhavali's case the OT assistant had replaced the suture materials in the OT. He was well equipped now. Yogendra and Hiroo were suturing the wound from the two ends and proceeding to the centre.

"Cut, sister."

"Sister, hold this with artery forceps and keep it straight."

"Okay, sister. Cut."

This went on for the next fifteen minutes. The anaesthesia was wearing off and the patient was getting restive and moving his legs. The last stitch, however, was in place.

After checking the vital parameters, we wheeled the patient on a trolley to the male ward. He was in pain and tonight didn't promise to be good. Especially since we had not been able to elucidate the cause. We had not identified anything. The mystery was still unresolved. We were at a loss and really worried. When the patient reposes such explicit faith in our abilities, the moral responsibility to help him recover multiplies and the endeavour to heal him is heightened.

It was my turn to do duty that night. After re-assessing his needs, I wrote his orders. Intravenous fluids, both saline and dextrose, with potassium in one and vitamins in the other. Antibiotics ..... Strepto-pen was stepped up to thrice daily .... an act of desperation. We had just opened and closed the abdomen, we had handled the intestine, we had put a needle into the spinal space, we had put our hands into the abdominal cavity. We had done so much, in a devitalised patient. Fearing severe infection I had instinctively upped the dose of antibiotics. I sat by the bedside for a few minutes watching over Potya and thinking. He seemed at ease and the treatment plan was set. He seemed to be sleeping. So when he showed no adverse signs for the next hour I decided to retire to my room. I asked the nurse to call me if there was any problem.

She was to check his abdominal girth every hour, along with his vital signs and urine output. I asked the nurse to send me a call at 5 am so that I could review the overnight progress. It was past midnight. I headed for the doctors' quarters with mixed feelings and trepidation.

25. Eosinophils and Recovery

Though I wanted to sleep, I was worried about the outcome of our latest intervention. Back in the room I found the others fast asleep. The day's excitement had taken its toll. I changed and stepped into the protective shadow of the mosquito net.

The next thing I realised was gentle knocking at the front door. I looked at my watch with blurred vision. The time was 5.15 am. My morning alarm.

"Coming."

I seemed to have slept through the last five hours. I must have been exhausted. Quickly changing into my trousers and shirt, I made for the wards. I was really anxious and keen to know what had transpired overnight.

Potya had fever. Understandable. The abdominal girth had come down by six centimetres and the abdomen was softer than yesterday. "Must have been due to the continuous aspiration of fluid by the Ryle's tube," I mused to myself. He was hydrated and his face had a fuller look. The stitches seemed to be fine. But.... the peristalsis were still absent. I noted my findings, and with a slight pang of disappointment, I moved away from the patient's bed. I was still not sure what would be the outcome of the heroic measures we had employed last night. We were still very much in the dark.

At the nurses' station I checked his reports and, on looking at the complete blood count, I noted that the differential count was slightly skewed, the eosinophil count being 20%, which was very high. I stared at it...deep in thought. I quickly calculated the absolute count. It was 2000 cells per cubic millimetre! This rang a bell. Didn't I learn on my ward rounds in Bombay that the eosinophil count at this level is significant for Tropical Eosinophilia? I made a mental note of bringing it up later. I finished my rounds in the next hour and was back in the room for the morning cup of tea. The boys were just surfacing at 6.30 am washed and ready for breakfast, I settled down on the top step of the house to watch the neighbourhood wake up.

Vahini arrived, bright and bubbly.

"Tea?" she asked.

"Yes!" I replied enthusiastically.

"Making." So saying, she stepped into the house and headed straight for the kitchen. The boys were ready by the time Vahini had the breakfast going. We sat down to enjoy it together.

We discussed Potya whilst we had breakfast, recounting and re- examining yesterday's events. I filled them in on the latest and, in passing, mentioned that he had a high eosinophil count. The significance of this count still didn't strike me. But then, nobody else could shed light on the significance either. We were soon to discover.

It was my duty at the OPD. Hiroo and I headed for the OPD and Yogendra was heading back home today. Dadan took rounds.

There were many patients so we just got down to work right away. Diarrhoea, cold, cough, fever, malaria, more fevers, injury on the shin (bleeding profusely) and many more patients. The last patient was sent to the minor OT for Dadan to stitch up. Dr. Dhande and Dadan attended to the patient and were busy with him for the next hour. It was close to noon and the OPD was almost done when I got an urgent call from the ward nurse, "Doctor! Hurry! Come soon. The patient is vomiting."

No sooner I received the call I was up and rushing to the male ward. There I saw Potya, standing, three steps away from his bed, near the edge of the railing, vomiting. He had vomited over the ledge of the corridor which skirted the male ward. He had already had a big vomit but it seemed that there was more to come. By the time I reached him and was able to look over the ledge, he had straightened up, and. to my immense horror, I saw two round worms in his mouth and one in his nostril. One look over the ledge and I saw at least twenty, wriggling round worms, still living! Never in my life had I seen such a sight. The diagnosis was now crystal clear. This was round worm infestation leading to intestinal obstruction.

I grabbed a rat-toothed forcep from the nurses tray and pulled out the worms from his mouth and nose. There were no more worms visible. He was in obvious pain from the effort of vomiting. I escorted him back to the bed and called the sweeper to clean up the mess. After I had gathered my wits and recovered from this shocking sight, I reassured Potya and told him that everything was going to be fine soon.

I headed, then, for the nurses station, where I asked her to acquire Mebendazole tablets from Vashani. He always kept them in stock, as worms were very common in this area. Why didn't we think of this possibility earlier? I started Potya on oral Mebendazole at that very moment. After the vomiting he was so much more comfortable. As there were no clear intestinal movements yet, I continued the intravenous drip. After settling him I returned to the OPD to finish seeing the patients waiting for me. The news of the worm vomit spread fast. Everyone in the hospital was happy. The pall of apprehension and dejection lifted and an air of optimism supervened.

26. Respite: Bonding Over Dinner

The rest of the day was uneventful. Dhavali's wound was gaping, but clean, and would take some time to heal. She needed daily care but there was no stress like there was earlier. Potya was much better. His Ryle's tube was still in place and intravenous fluids were continued. His progress was excellent. His distension was much better, the abdomen was softer and his temperature was normal. There had been a patient with a snake bite, but there were no adverse signs of poisoning. We gave him a dose of anti snake venom and decided to keep him under observation. The rest of the ward was quiet.

We actually looked forward to a peaceful and relaxed dinner today. We hadn't enjoyed this kind of respite for a while. Every day was an adventure and there was always some anxiety that weighed on our minds.

Vahini had cooked something extra today. She was sympathetic to our plight and had watched us, for the past two weeks, working hard without respite. We planned on having a 'banquet' tonight.

Which meant a whole meal and hopefully some dessert.

Back in the room, it was Dadan, Hiroo and me. We had so much to talk about and so many stories to tell, thoughts to share, and experiences to discuss. After a long while we were light hearted and free to enjoy our meal in peace. After the events of the past two weeks, we felt a sense of relief and also a sense of fulfilment......
of having done something meaningful. We had EARNED our respite. My colleagues confirmed that the past two weeks had seen

more action at the hospital than the past two months had seen. We had done two surgeries and both, in their own rights, were difficult surgeries, not routinely performed at the cottage hospital. After the surgeries we had stood through the consequences, with precious little infrastructure to lean on. No investigations, no sophisticated drugs, no incubators, no team of experts to consult, no experience, no ....no ....no.... 'No' to so many things...! Yet.... We had many a 'yes' on our side. Yes..to courage, yes,... to patience, yes to innovation, yes to the feeling of wanting to help someone in distress at any cost. AT ANY COST!!! Yes... To being ready to sacrifice sleep, hunger, mental peace, and personal gain to do someone some good. Yes.... to being prepared to go through hard times, wilfully.

In the city, during the urban phase of our internship, we had gone through hard times. We had worked through many nights, we had been through many life and death situations. We had been in the blood and gore. Yet, in the city, we were the absolute bottom rung on the ladder. We made no decisions, we did no surgeries, we did no procedures. We did as we were told. On the other hand, in this rural setting, we made decisions, we did procedures, we did surgeries, we took the initiative, we stood by our decisions, we were responsible for what we did. We had to use every resource at our disposal here and the resources were very few. We lived by our wits, our instincts, and sheer determination. The books were of no use. The practice of Medicine in the villages is something beyond normal imagination. Nothing in the world challenges your wits and instincts the way rural medicine does. Nowhere in the world do you see genuine simplicity, gratitude and contentment, as one sees in a poor villager. No one can match the tenacity, grit and loyalty of an Adivasi villager.

Dinner was ready. We filled our plates in the kitchen and brought them out to the table in the ante room. It was a pleasant night and, for a change, it was a clear day. Gentle clouds, not the heavy nimbus, as in the last two weeks. Today the climate was in keeping with our mood. Relaxed and happy. Glad that things were going well. Glad that we were being accepted at this hospital and the town, too. Glad that we all had a lovely working relationship with no maladjustments or clash of opinions. Every viewpoint was respected, evaluated, employed in unanimous spirit. We shared the work without as much as a creak or a groan. Our rural stint promised to be the finest part of our medical education.

Dinner was rotis, french beans, and potato vegetable, dal and rice, lemon pickle and papad. This, apparently, is a run-of-the-mill menu describing the everyday meal in an average household. What is so banquet-ish about this menu? When we were eating roti and vegetables for lunch and dal and rice for dinner, and most of the times this food was eaten in stress and on the run, then today's hot and complete meal eaten in a relaxed mood was, indeed, a treat for kings!

"This is really good, guys."

"Really."

"Haven't eaten like this for so long!"

"This papad......It's good yar! Where from?"

"There's this old lady, who has been coming to the OPD for treatment. I've got to know her well now. She told me she specialises in making ragi papads. She is noble and sweet- tempered, she is widowed and has no kids. She does this to make some money to eke out a living.......just thought I'd help her out by buying some."

"What's her name?"

"Oak-bai. Mrs. Shashikala Oak. Every one calls her Oak-bai."

Apparently, she had been very ill and was admitted, at some point in time, in our hospital when a previous batch of interns were here. She recovered, and thereafter she gifted that batch of interns with her signature nachani (ragi) papads. They were an instant hit, and ever since, these papads have been everyone's favourites. They helped enhance the meal, no matter what was cooked.

"You know where she stays? I'd like to buy some more and take them to Bombay. I'm sure they would love this taste."

"Nahin yaar. This tastes good here because there is nothing else to eat. It tastes good because we work so hard and we are so hungry. At home, toh, we get food without lifting a finger! Free mein khana milta hai."

Yes. In Bombay things are different. We are spoilt for choice and have problems with abundance, whereas, here the food is frugal and simple, so when there is a little beyond bare minimum, it's a grand fiesta.

"Baba, just enjoy them whilst you are here. When we go we'll think of carrying some to Bombay."

"I want to meet her all the same."

"Me too."

There are so many such people in the village and town of Jawhar who do these small things that not only win your heart, but also give them a source of earnest livelihood.

"You know Mukne? That brat of a watchman.?"

"Of course!"

"He has a unique side business. He makes whips."

"Yes. I know about that. I asked him to make me one," I said rather sheepishly. "I'm going to learn from him how to use it before going back from here."

"Why do you want to learn how to use a whip? Something special?"

"You don't know? It's a full scale martial art. He does it so well. Just like Bruce Lee."

"Oh, so you want to be Bruce Lee, huh?"

"No, no! But, what's the harm in learning some martial art? Any problem?"

"Learn, learn, no problem. Just don't beat up someone for nothing."

"I'll beat you first! Just for practice!"

Banter continued as the meal progressed.

"Here, have some more roti. Vegetables are in that vessel. Take it."

"Pass the pickle."

"Hey! Dessert Kya hai? What's for dessert? Not cucumber I hope?"

I was surprised at the mention of cucumber as a dessert. I asked,"Why do you say that? Something happened?"

"Arrey, Anand! You don't know. You were in London."

"What happened? Tell me."

"You know how many Adivasis come to us every day. You know how poor they are. And how much they lose when they leave home to come to us for help. Well, despite these hardships, after they have recovered, they would come to us at the time of discharge and sheepishly, they would untie a small cloth bundle and take out from it a large cucumber, grown in their own farm, fresh as fresh can be, and gift it to us!"

"That's so kind of them."

"For all these days, we have been having cucumber for dessert. It was the best thing available and cheap! Doobta Kya Nahin Khata!" This was said with a devious grin of fake altruism. There was, however, a grain of truth in this story. It is true that Adivasis, once healed and ready to go home, always show their gratitude in some way or the other. Giving the produce of their land is probably the most noble way of expressing gratitude and, I dare say, worth more than a million bucks any day!

"You have changed the whole Muhavra, Dadan!..... It is...Doobta Kya Nahin Karta!"

"Nahin re! ...okay I'll change it....... Marta Kya Nahin Khata!!!!"

"Ha ha ha haa! Drama king!!!"

"Okay guys, really! What's for dessert?"

"Jelly, jelly, jelly!! Rex Jelly!"

"Hahahaha.... Now say......Ting tong!!! Just like the ad."

"Where did it come from?"

"Mom packed some for us when I was returning. I was resisting at first, but she kept saying that when you are there you will need it."

"So here we are, enjoying jelly in the wilderness. Thanks yaar!"

"My Mom makes jelly with custard. Tastes delicious."

"That's life, yaar! Jelly, then no custard. Custard, then no jelly!!"

"Did anybody ever get everything?"

Dinner was done, and the night had moved on. It was past midnight.

"Good night guys. I'm going to sleep. Can't tell when we will have to wake up for some sick guy."

So true. Any moment of restful sleep, any meal eaten in peace, any opportunity for respite,..... just grab it!!! You don't know when you will lose that moment, that opportunity, that joy! Life here was a serious of uncertainties. As they say of Cricket....Glorious Uncertainties.

27. Blood!

It must have been 4 am. I was in bed. Not a sound outside. I don't know why my eyes opened, as though it was morning, and it was time to wake up. I checked the time in my watch, and was just contemplating whether to get out of bed, or to sleep some more, when there was a sharp knock on the door.

"Yes!?"

"Sir! Sir, snake bite! Quick!"

"Yeto. Coming." How short-lived peace can be. Here we were, just thinking of our relaxed meal last night, and how we would sleep well tonight.......But here was the next adventure presenting itself to us. As his bed was near the door, like me, Dadan had also heard the knock and had gotten out of his bed. Amongst all of us, he was the more experienced one with the treatment of snakebites. It was reassuring to have him come along with me. This would be my second case in two days. Snake bite cases needed urgent care. So we were out of our beds in a jiffy and were on our way to the ward in two minutes.

In the female ward, there was this Adivasi girl looking really toxic. She was bleeding from her mouth, nose and with petechiae and purpuric patches all over the body. She had been bitten by a snake yesterday and they had taken almost ten hours to reach us.

"Sister, bring a normal saline drip and the anti snake venom (ASV) fast!"

You, Sister, bring a bowl of water and another empty bowl. Make her gargle and clean the blood from her mouth." Both sisters were on the job now. We, meanwhile, examined the patient for the tell- tale fang marks that one often sees. We spotted the fang marks on her shin amidst the multitude of purpuric patches. There was swelling at the site of the fang marks. This snake was a viper! The toxin of a viper leads to excessive bleeding and, if not attended to in time, the bleeding could involve vital areas like the brain, lungs and intestines.

We started the drip and let it flow at full speed. The needle being a wide bore, number 18, which allowed the fluid to stream in. Hydrating the patient was of paramount importance. As soon as the ASV arrived, we attached it to the intravenous line and injected it very slowly. We stopped after half a millilitre had gone in. This was the test dose. At times, when the patient is hypersensitive to this medication a large dose can be life-threatening, because it can cause a massive reaction leading to death. Hence ASV demands a test dose and, only after there is no adverse reaction, should the rest of the dose be given. After watching her for any adverse reaction for 5 minutes, when there was none, we injected the rest of the dose over ten minutes. This was about 20 ccs. We put another 40 ccs of the ASV in the drip which was set to flow over the next 40 minutes.

She had bled extensively, but there was no evidence of any bleeding in her brain or lungs. She had not yet passed urine so there was no way we could tell whether she had bled in her kidneys. That remained to be seen. There was no overt evidence of bleeding in the gastrointestinal tract either. If she were to bleed in her gastrointestinal tract it would manifest as blood in the vomitus or in the stools.

The fluid was going smoothly and the bottle was nearly empty.

"Sister, bring another normal saline drip and add 40 cc of ASV to it." Meanwhile I collected a sample of blood for a complete blood count. This would be done in the morning. The patient was stable. I engaged her in conversation to distract her mind from the seemingly terrifying situation she was in. The second drip was also coming to an end and her BP was now, 100/60 mmHg. She looked a lot better with the hydration.

"How did this happen," I asked her.

"I was going to start cooking dinner for my family. Just before starting to cook, I thought, maybe, first, I should fetch some water for the storage tank, as the tank at home had very little water. We need to fill water from the well nearby regularly, so I gathered the vessels and walked over to the well. The grass around the well had grown so much. In some spots it is as high as three feet. My man has had no time to cut the grass, as he was busy picking green chillies to sell in the Friday market. If he missed this Friday, he would have to wait till next Friday, and the chillies would turn red.

"So when I went to fill water at the well, I had to step into the grass to reach the pulley. Just then, something very sharp hit me on my leg. I screamed and jumped back. I saw the snake going away as I moved back. Maybe I had stepped on it or something. Thereafter I can't remember what happened. I was scared. My husband came running out and saw the fear and pain on my face. He shouted for his brother from the next farm and they both helped me back home.

"I saw the mark on my leg and told them that it was already swelling. My husband said that we would have to go to the hospital for further treatment.......but there was no vehicle to take us. The next bus was at ten in the morning. So. He asked his brother to come along and, taking turns to carry me on their backs, they brought me to the hospital.

"Doctor, I am so tired! Am I going to die? I have little children. Tell me doctor, am I going to die?" Her tired, desperate eyes, pleaded an answer from me. I averted her gaze. I had no answer for her, as I didn't know myself.

"Sister. The second drip is also going to finish. Please bring another one with 40 cc of ASV. And let it flow for 40 minutes. And sister, see if she wants to pass urine. I want to see the colour."

I continued avoiding her gaze as I kept sizing the situation, hoping that I had not missed anything important. As per the books, extensive bleeding after a bite from the Viper is pre-imminently fatal. Yet, with limited means we had to save her. The book said transfuse plasma or whole blood in case of such extensive bleeding. Hell!! Where do I get fresh plasma and fresh blood in this God-forsaken village.!! It is indeed ironical,...the city hospital has all these facilities but no cases of snake bite, and in the village, where the snakes bite, the hospitals have no means to treat. When the snake bites its victim in a remote village, even the means of transport to bring the hapless victim to a treatment centre is unavailable. Precious time is lost in bringing the patient to the hospital. Regardless of the ground realities, we had to move on.

We were the unfortunate, ill-equipped frontline.

This girl was going to go home if we could help it.

28. Damn the Books!

"Look. Don't worry. You are going to be fine." I reassured her, hoping against hope that I was right. The urine was clear, indicating no bleeding in the kidneys. She was passing urine freely. There was no confusion or neurological deficit to suggest internal bleeding in the brain. We were still not in the red!

She was cause for concern, so we kept by her bedside, changing the treatment as the situation warranted. We monitored her personally, taking turns to do so. If there was a one percent chance of survival it was going to be her's!

Thus far we had only attended to the patient. We had not talked to the husband and his brother, who were quietly sitting in a corner, fear writ large on their countenance. We offered them some water and asked them to eat something. They looked exhausted. Despite all my coaxing and convincing, and reassuring them that we were standing vigil over this girl and that they were free to go and eat something, they would not budge from her bedside.

Dawn was breaking and the other patients were waking up. The nurses who had worked with us in the night were getting ready to leave, and the new ones had arrived and were being filled in on the night's developments. The girls had a system of 'giving over, taking over' after every shift change, which ensured seamless care of the patient, regardless of which nurse cared for her. The urine sample was yellow. There was no overt bleeding but the possibility couldn't be ruled out. Our only bet was to hydrate her adequately, providing a free flow of urine which would prevent any blood from obstructing urine flow and damaging the kidneys.

The fourth drip of saline was about to be started. 140 cc of ASV had been administered. We still didn't know what to expect. We had planned on 200cc in the first two hours and then 100cc after 6 hours, if needed. The blood in her nose had coagulated. I dared not dislodge it for fear of causing a fresh bout of bleeding. I told her not to pick her nose, and told the girls not to dislodge or clean the clot unless I asked them to do so. There was some oozing of blood from her gums and when she coughed, her sputum was blood tinged. It seemed like she had bled everywhere!

"Sister, add another 60 cc of ASV to the current drip." She looked at me quizzically, asking with her eyes....Are you sure? Isn't it too much? It was too much by the books. But. this was hard reality.

And I had a patient running out of time. She was young, she was innocent, she deserved the best. The situation we were in, was precarious. We had no facility to transfuse blood, we had no ventilator, we had no ICU like in the big hospitals. We just had our common sense, our wits, our courage, and our frugal medications.

I shook out of my reverie and exclaimed, "Sister. Damn the books! Just give it!"

She returned to the nursing station to bring the ASV. Dadan had returned to the room to get ready for the day. He had sent word that I should join them for breakfast. How could I? This girl was alone and needed close monitoring. I told the ward boy to tell them that unless one of them came over I couldn't leave this girl.

The bleeding from the nose and gums seemed to have stopped. The second sample of urine was white, ruling out any bleeding within the kidneys. Good news! The lab results were still awaited. We continued with active hydration and added Streptopen twice a day. The wound on her leg could fester, the multiple interventions we had done could introduce infection, and the hospital could have given her some infection. In order to pre-empt this possibility we started the antibiotic. There was no room for even a single step backwards.

When I examined her again she was asleep. She looked well hydrated, her pulse and respiration were normal, and she had no fever. The nose bleed and the gum bleeds had settled and no active bleeding spots were identifiable. She must have been so terrified throughout the long trek to the hospital and the sight of blood must have taken all hope away. After reassuring her, and after she felt better with the fluids and medication, she had succumbed to the safety of sleep. Her husband and his brother had also stretched out in the corridor and were fast asleep.

29. A Happy Routine

The fourth drip was on flow, 200 cc of ASV would have been administered by the time this drip was done, the urine output was good, the oral and nasal bleeding had stopped for the time being and she was fast asleep. I thought it was safe to leave her for a short time to go and wash up and get some food.

My breakfast was waiting for me on the table. The tea was cold. Never mind. When I returned to the ward Hiroo was taking rounds. He informed me that Dhavali's white cell count, done three days ago, was still 13,000/cmm. Her antibiotics were being continued but she needed more protein. Though she was eating better, she would need supplements.

"Let's get her some Horlicks from the grocery in the market. Or else, let's buy her some peanuts and she can have about 100gms a day. Maybe when her protein levels improve she will heal." We made a mental note to add this new item to our already strained budget....but it was of paramount importance.

Potya had passed a liquid stool today. His peristaltic activity had resumed and that meant his intestines had fully recovered. This was great news. The stool did not contain round worms. Maybe future stool samples would show some more worms. The sounds of peristalsis were loud and clear, so we decided to start him on oral liquids. For the first hour he would receive only sips of water. Thereafter, if well tolerated, we would add clear soup, thin dal, and rice kanji (a warm gruel of rice). Potya was getting better. He, of his own accord, had got off his bed and was taking a small walk in the corridor. He looked like he was at peace with himself, and he was actually smiling today.

Yesterday's snake bite case was ready for discharge. Today's girl. Laxmi, as we had found her name to be, was also comfortable and still asleep. I had instructed the nurses to give her clear liquids when she woke up. She seemed to be on the track to recovery.... yet, it was too soon to celebrate.

There is this test wherein we tie the blood pressure cuff on the forearm and inflate the cuff to a pressure of 80 mmHg.. After a minute we release the cuff and look for purpuric patches. If there are more patches then the snake venom had not been adequately neutralised. Which meant we needed to give more ASV. This test is the Hess test. On seeing her resting, I decided to visit her in the afternoon. She was being closely watched by four nurses, three interns and Dr. Dhande, who had also seen her and he had given us a nice compliment saying, "Well done boys! Well managed."

The OPD was busy as usual. We saw more than 50 patients of diverse diseases. I had to admit two cases of fever and three cases of gastroenteritis. They would all receive adequate hydration and streptopen, and they would all respond to the treatment. There were three deliveries scheduled for tonight. One for each of us.

After OPD, I headed for Laxmi's bed. She was awake. Her routine urine showed some 50 red blood cells per high power field and there was some protein present too. Her white cell count was 12,500/ cmm and her haemoglobin was 8 gms%. The technician had visually assessed the platelets and they were on the lower limit of normal. She was not out of the woods yet. As she was tolerating oral fluids, I put her on a soft diet with plenty of fluids. The intravenous fluids would continue with the next drip carrying in it's substance 50 cc of ASV over the next three hours. We would reassess thereafter.

I did the Hess test on her at 2 pm. The test showed new purpuric patches informing us that the dangers had not passed. We must continue the same treatment and watch assiduously for any new haemorrhages at any other sites or any bleeding from the nose or the mouth. By afternoon the patients in the wards were stable and the OPD had been dealt with. None of the pregnant women were ready for delivery. And they wouldn't be ready till 7 pm.

Later in the afternoon. Dr Dhande was going to conduct the vasectomy camp. Vasectomy surgeries were his favourites, he would do thirty or so in one session. He fairly flew through so many patients in a blur of action. His speed of finding the vas, tying it, cutting it, and closing the wound was incredible. He would finish each case in record time. The assistant intern would find this blur of action very difficult to deal with, and would invariably get lost.

30. A Plain Day

After a busy, yet fruitful morning, we had all settled for lunch.

"How much ASV did you use for Laxmi, Anand?"

"I used 200 ccs so far and now 50 ccs are going in a slow drip."

"Too much, no?"

"Yes, I know. She looked like she was sinking, so I took a chance. I know the dose was very high but....I thought if she bled like this continuously it would be too little, too late. I just went by my instincts."

"I've seen many snake bite cases, but never so bad. She was bleeding so much. Thank God she has stabilised."

"She has bled in her kidneys too. The urine showed RBCs."

"Hope she's turned the corner."

"Dr. Dhande saw her. He was mighty pleased with the outcome."

"Hmmm..."

"Even Potya is doing well. He's had a few 'loosies' today but I think that's a good sign. His gut has resumed work." I said, with a wry smile. "He walked in the corridor too. On his own. He is a tough guy!"

"That's great!"

"I'm tired, guys. I'm going to take a nap. We have those deliveries tonight. Who knows how long they will take. Better sleep whilst we can. Wake me, please. Five?"

"Sure, sleep."

Post lunch, Hiru went to the minor OT, whilst Dadan and I turned in for the much needed nap. Sleep was something that evaded us all the time. If we ever believed that life at the cottage hospital could be structured and disciplined we couldn't have been further from the truth. In fact, whoever worked here was awake all the time.

Either he was working, or he was sitting at home and worrying about a sick patient. The commitment became so strong, and the sense of responsibility so heightened, that one was completely immersed in his work. Nothing else mattered. Life was work, work and more work....and sometimes food!

At five, Vahini woke us up with a cup of tea. It was so good to have slept. I wouldn't have been able to stay up another night if I hadn't. After tea we returned to the hospital for rounds. The labour ward was still quiet. The contractions were coming, few and far between. It almost felt that all three women were going to deliver at the same time. They were walking around the ward to encourage the onset of labour pains.

Dhavali was getting better gradually. There was a little soakage in the dressing so I changed it, she was eating better, she was more mobile and her spirit was so much better than when she had just come to the hospital. She was showing more interest in her environment and had conversations with other women in the ward.

"What do you think she feels when she sees other women delivering normal babies?"

"She must be feeling bad from within. It must be a sordid reminder of her hugh loss."

"I can't say she is jealous. She is not that kind. She is too soft for that. But... Remorse,..regret, something like....bitterness?"

"Ya, maybe. Can't really say what goes on in her mind. If I was in her place, I'd feel terrible."

"Do you think shifting her to the female ward would help? Keeping her away from the maternity ward? You think not seeing the babies will help her to forget her trauma?"

"It can work both ways. In the female ward she will see women much worse off than her. This may help her to count her own blessings and thus aid her return to normalcy on the other hand......". I paused to weigh my thoughts, "On the other hand....She may be terrified if she saw the snake bite case or other seriously ill patients and that may push her into further depression....don't know."

"Let her be. She is fine where she is!"

"Let's just aim at getting her home soon. That's the best place for her."

Potya was ready for a full meal. He was asking for food.

"No. We must not hurry. Wait a day before giving him a full meal. Or else he may relapse and feel terrible."

When informed that he would get a full meal in the morrow he ruefully smiled his resigned acceptance in the delay in seeing real food. He probably slept that night dreaming of food. His appetite must have returned in vengeance now that the worms had been dealt with in full measure.

Laxmi, too, was cheerful. Though she looked haggard and pale, blotches of subcutaneous haemorrhage had caused a patchy pattern all over her body, making her look hideous. Nevertheless, the oral bleeding had stopped, and the nostrils were encrusted with dry blood, signifying no further bleeding. Her abdomen was soft and there was no evidence of bleeding in the brain or kidneys. The urine had become light yellow and was clear. She was taking oral fluids comfortably, so we could start her on a full diet from tomorrow.

"Shall we go to the market? We could get a breather and get some supplies as well."

"You and Hiroo go. I'll stay on call." Dadan said.

"Okay."

31. The Market Place

It was 6.30 pm when Hiroo and I left for the market place. The market place was a small place with vegetable vendors, farmers selling fresh ware, food stalls, some selling snacks, and some selling other knick-knacks. There was one grocery store. They sold everything one could ever want!

We first went to the vegetable and fruit vendor. The vendors all knew Hiroo.

"Doctor saab. Come to my stall. Here, take these bhindis, they are fresh. And see these brinjals, they are polished and shining. And some mirchi? Limes?

Another vendor, "Arrey doctor! See my vegetables. Beans, tomatoes, cucumbers. I have all......Come, come!"

Hiroo braced himself to bargain. He asked me what I wished to buy. "Shall we pick up some beans, some tomatoes, and bhindi ......and......."

"Anand, we are in Jawhar, not Bombay. You don't buy so much all at once...we buy for one or two days, or else it will spoil. We don't have a fridge." Looking towards the vendor he asked,"How much?"

"Sixty rupees."

Hiroo turned to go, saying, "No! Too much." He beckoned to me to come to the next vendor. I was amused with his play acting and was smiling broadly.

"Okay, Sir. Fifty-five?"

"No." Hiru walked away two more paces towards the next vendor.

"Okay last, fifty rupees." Now we were both smiling. The vendor, too smiled in mock resignation. We payed him fifty rupees and moved on. Hiroo was explaining to me the ways of the world as applicable in Jawhar. The ways that he had picked up in the last two months. He explained to me why we could only buy two days stock of fruit and vegetable because, without refrigeration, the produce would spoil and will have to be thrown away. This will lead to a lot of waste which would stretch our budget. I realised that in Jawhar we will not only learn medicine, we would also learn 'thrift', which is a hugh lesson in life.

"Anand, at first you will get a culture shock in this village. You have just come from the city, and moreover, not from Bombay, you have come here almost directly from London. The poverty, the simplicity, the slow life, the laid back people and most of all, the silence will take you some time to get used to."

I was listening to Hiroo and weighing his words in my mind. There was a slight culture shock on the first day when I had arrived with a heart loaded with fear. There had been a pang, albeit momentary, that had me regretting my decision of taking up this post.

However, my talk with Dr. Dhande on the first day, dispelled all those doubts instantaneously. After that initial fear there had been no looking back and hospital life had got me involved cent percent. No! I had no regrets, no qualms. No culture shock anymore. In fact I was extremely happy. I was enjoying this experience to the hilt and undoubtedly the experience was enriching my life.

"Do we need anything from the grocery store?"

"Yes. We need to buy peanuts for Dhavali." We bought them.

"I'm buying some bananas," Hiru said, and picked up three bananas for us.

We turned to head home as it was quite dark now and, here in Jawhar, after sundown, very rapidly every one packs up and heads home. The streets would soon be deserted. Deep in thought, we started our short trek back home.

32. An Exquisite Spectacle

We were slowly making our way back to the hospital. The roads were ill-lit and there were no street lights. Normally if you were out in the dark you carried a torch but, not being used to this, we had not carried ours. The road was bathed in the dim, silvery moonlight of the half moon, the sound of crickets pervaded the air and far in the distance I could see the silhouette of the dome of our hospital atop the hill with the dim light glowing inside the building.

All of a sudden, I stopped in my tracks! On the dark road and in the dim light I saw at least a hundred little blue lights on the ground. These lights were moving, glowing, a fluorescent blue, like small dots on the ground. I was transfixed and momentarily speechless. I just stopped and looked with awe. Hiroo, realising that I was not by his side, stopped and looked back,"What happened?"

"Hiroo! Look! Glow worms!! Can't believe it?" As though mesmerised, I stood there on the road just looking at these creatures, awestruck. This was the first time in my life I had seen glow worms. I had, hitherto, only read about these little magnificent creatures. The caravan of glow worms seemed endless. The entire road seemed to be filled with them. I stood there for a good five minutes, enamoured. "Come on, Anand, you will see them every day till you get tired of them."

Reluctantly, I moved forward. Still lost in the world of glow worms. Taking in the sight of hundreds of little blue lights moving on the dark road. The feeling of awe remained with me for a long, long time.

We got back to the hospital and found Dadan in the room. Vahini was cooking some dinner and the smells emanating from the kitchen were very appetising.

"Let's eat while the going is good."

"Lets,"

"Dadan, glow worm dekha! Saw so many glow worms."

"Achha! We have seen millions of them. Every day we used to see them, especially if we go out of the hospital at night. At first, we were also excited to see them. But now,...Got used to them."

"But... They are amazing. How Nature creates so many things... it's incredible, isn't it?"

"Anand, just study the walls of our bedroom at night and you will see at least a hundred different insects, all masterpieces of creation."

You're right! Every night I look at them and marvel. The dragon fly is the most beautiful. The wings are diaphanous, so intricately designed and so delicate."

"Ya, I was looking at that insect for so long on my first night after you left."

"You mean 'absconded' from here!" and we all burst into laughter on being reminded of the frightful word used, for my sudden disappearance, by the Dean's office.

"Those days I didn't get sleep. I was so scared of those creepy crawlies! God knows which disease they could spread."

"I don't think I have had the time to feel scared. Firstly, I'm so tired by the time we sleep that I don't see them at all. Secondly, I realise that if you guys aren't scared then there is no reason for me to be.

"You are right. It's only on the first day that you nurture fear of these magnificent creatures. From the next day, it's just AWE! The sight of them never ceases to make you stop in wonder.. Wonder how Nature created so many beautiful creatures, so much variety, so much diversity, so many different designs, so many different functions I can't stop wondering."

"Hmmmmm,.Yes, it's so true that the diversity and richness of Nature in this area is, by far, the most beautiful in comparison with any other place I may have been to."

There was no news from the labour ward even after we had finished our dinner. We sat up talking to each other before, one by one, we all drifted off into deep sleep.

The days take their toll. Sleep heals like nothing else.

33. Labour of Love

"Sir! Labour!" The voice at the door proclaimed.

Startled by the sharp knock on the door and the urgency in the voice, I jumped out of bed in a moment. I pushed into my slippers and headed straight for the labour ward. Loud screams from the direction of the labour ward were indicative of the frenetic activity in the ward..... And understandably. three girls were in labour at once. My steps hastened and I entered the labour ward only to find two of the nurses attending to two of the prospective mothers who were both in an advanced state of labour at the same time.

Fortunately, the other patients were stable, hence there was no pressure on the girls from the general ward. Maushi was attending to one of the patients and Neelima was watching over the other girl. One look at the third and I was sure she would be a close next on the list of deliveries.

I approached Maushi's patient first. Reassured her with a pat on her head, telling her to be calm. I put the fetoscope on the abdomen to check the fetal heart sounds. "Good. 140/minute." She was fine. I moved to the second girl and did the same. Neelima assured me that she had just checked the fetal heart rate and found it to be 110/minute. Good.

"Maushi, Cervix?"

"Fully dilated. Head is descending." So she was going to be first to deliver. As the uterus spasm-ed, the pain escalated and the girl let out a scream! At the same time Maushi, Neelima, and the ward maid all yelled in encouragement, "PUSH!!!" The girl's face contorted in a grimace and she took a deep breath and pushed hard. Her breath held, and strain writ large on her face, was a sight to behold. The trio of nurses kept up their encouragement, "PUSH!!! PUSH!!! Come on ! PUSH!!"

"The baby is crowning. Come on!! Push!! Just a little left!" The girl let go of her breath, panted for a bit and then, again took in a lung full of air, grimaced and pushed for all she was worth. Maushi was feverishly ironing the vagina with two fingers and facilitating the head to move down in synchrony with the push of the uterine contractions. Another five seconds and one more full-blooded push and the head was out. "Push!! Last time!" A deep breath, a strained scream and a last push, Maushi had hooked her finger under the baby's arm and pulled the shoulder out, and then, in one rush, the other shoulder, the body and the legs popped out. There was a short pause. A momentary silence. Maushi held the baby by the ankles and slapped it on the back a few times sharply and there was the yelp followed by a lusty cry that broke the expectant hush.

The labour ward maid took the baby and placed it on a green sheet of cloth and exclaimed,"It's a boy!" the mother's tired and anxious face transformed to joy in a flash. The pain, the fatigue, the apprehension and the fear, all dissolved in that one magical moment. There was a smile on every face.

I examined the child for any abnormalities. There is a protocol which has been in use for years, and will continue to be used, as long as clinical medicine is practiced. A new born child is examined for five parameters and is given a score which decides whether he is normal or will need help to become normal. The APGAR score is a sum of five different parameters which are two marks each. The respiratory rate, the heart rate, the skin colour, the reflexes, and the muscle tone, each of these parameters are given marks 0, 1 or 2.

The best score for a normal child is a perfect ten. In case of discrepancies in the above parameters the score may be lower. This child was a perfect ten!

By the time I had examined the child, Maushi and Neelima had moved to the second girl. Her screams rent the air, and encouraged by the smooth delivery she had just witnessed, she was already bearing down in unison with her uterine contractions.

"Sir, head is halfway down the birth canal. She will deliver in a few minutes. Can you please watch the placenta?" she said, looking in the direction of the first mother. I nodded and moved over to the foot end of the delivery bed. The cut end of the cord hung loosely. I quickly donned a pair of gloves and took hold of the cord. As i applied slight traction on it, it started to slip out. I exerted a steady traction and gradually the placenta, in one intact piece, was delivered. I smiled at the girl signifying that it was all done and that she was free to rest a while. I placed the placenta in a tray and asked the maid to drape the patient with a sheet and wrap the baby in a white sheet after duly washing him.

On the next bed, the chorus of, "PUSH!! PUSH!!" coupled with short screams and sounds of straining culminated in the birth of another boy. The lusty cries of the baby rent the air almost immediately. He scored a perfect ten, cherubic, and energetically moving his limbs.

Maushi and Neelima looked tired, but wore the most winsome smiles on their faces. The general atmosphere in the labour ward was one of elation. The birth of a new life was always a moment to celebrate.

I had been here for over an hour now and the time was 4.30am. The first two deliveries were done and one more to go. Neelima checked the patient's vitals and listened for the fetal heart sounds. All normal. The labour was progressing but she was not yet in full contraction. The patient was looking tired and very anxious. She was anticipating delivery since the previous morning and was now tiring. Her lips looked dry, "Sister, start a 5% dextrose saline drip at 30 drops per minute. Please keep a watch on the fetal heart sounds. I'm writing my notes and coming back."

At the nursing station Maushi was easing her tired bones. She said to the ward boy who was idling, "Aye Mama, thodishi chah banavsheel? Will you make some tea?"

He got up to go to the pantry, glad that he had something to do.

"Make for everyone," I said.

"Sure," he said with a broad grin on his face. He pumped the stove and soon had it going. Before long, the aroma of brewing tea filled the nurses' station. I had finished making my notes on the two deliveries. Just then Neelima walked in. Her face lit up when she smelled the tea. She grabbed a chair and sat down.

"Wow, tea! I sure could do with some. I have chocolate biscuits. You want?" Neelima said with a twinkle in her eyes. One could never be sure when Neelima was pulling your leg or when she was serious. Chocolate biscuits with tea at 5am was, indeed, difficult to believe. Like a dream that would never realise.

Knowing this, I still played along, "Yes, of course." And lo and behold!! She pulled out a packet of chocolate biscuits from the drawer. I couldn't believe it. I hadn't set eyes on chocolate biscuits for a month. No time, no inclination, no money.

"Neelima, where did you get these biscuits from? Is it your birthday? Or something special?"

"No! Just felt like eating."

"Neelima, you did the hard work, you eat. Give Maushi some."

"Have one at least."

"Okay, just one, with the tea."

Neelima was a clean-hearted, lively, witty, and loving girl who worked very hard and was very dependable. I had never once heard her refusing to work or shirking a responsibility because no one was watching. In fact, all the nurses were like that but she was the liveliest. She was fun. With her constant prattle going on, there was never a dull moment.

"Neelima, thanks for the biscuit ! You eat." So saying, I got up to go and see the last girl waiting to deliver her baby.

She had sustained contractions and the head was engaged, but she was tiring. I could see maternal fatigue setting in. If this labour prolonged any more we would lose her cooperation and that could cause complications. I thought for a moment and then called out to Neelima. "Start a Pitocin drip. And watch the contractions." She added the Pitocin to the dextrose drip already on flow. In half an hour the girl's cervix was fully dilated and the head was lowering towards the outlet. Loud screams, calls to push, words of encouragement spurred the girl to, very soon, bring out the baby.

No matter how many deliveries I may have witnessed, the wonder of child birth never ceased to amaze me. It was nothing short of miraculous. She had delivered a baby girl with an APGAR score of a perfect ten. It was her first child and she was overjoyed.

After the notes were written I headed back to the room feeling rather circumspect and satisfied with the morning's work. The world had just been enriched by three beautiful lives.

34. Hema

Hiroo and Dadan were just waking up. Vahini, after hearing that I had just returned to the room after three deliveries, followed me to the room and asked me if I was ready for tea and breakfast. Since all of us were, she set about her work in the kitchen. I settled on the doorstep, and within moments, Hema came and sat down beside me. I have not alluded to her yet. Hema was Hemant's best friend.

Hemant was going to return in a couple of days and Hiroo was going to take some time off. Hemant, whilst he was here in the early part of our posting, had befriended Hema and shared his meals with her, fondled her, pampered her, loved her. In fact, we don't know what her name was before we came, but Hemant had christened her with her new name, Hema. Hema was the adopted village canine who had taken a fondness for our group, but was closest to Hemant. She would be at the doorstep every morning, and in the evening till we were all in the room. If, per chance, we were out in the wards, she would be on the doorstep waiting for us. She never had demands, she just came for the proximity, for the love, that she received unconditionally from all of us. If we fed her she was happy. If we couldn't because we were busy in the wards, she would forage around and look after herself. She was loyal and loving. It had become part of our daily need to spend a few moments with her. The need for intimacy was mutual. We needed her as much as she thrived in our company.

Whilst breakfast was being cooked, Dadan came and sat next to us. He asked,"Where did you go? Deliveries? Done?"

"Yes. Done. Two normals and one with the help of Pitocin. Normal were both boys and the Pitocin kid was a baby girl. All of them are so sweet and healthy."

We sat there on the steps contemplating our own thoughts. Hema sitting peacefully between us. Just basking in the feeling of belonging.

"You know, Dadan. These Adivasis........tenacity, grit, resilience..... Second nature to them. They look malnourished, weak, but when it comes to endurance, nobody can beat them. Now just look...... These three deliveries. They pushed. It must have hurt,... they may have been tired,....but no. They won't give up"

"True, Anand. That's because they face so many hardships, and have so little by way of luxury, that they develop grit and resilience. They have to survive amidst heavy odds. Predators, diseases, climatic vagaries, cold, heat, rain, unpredictable crops, thefts, and so many more situations that we can't even imagine."

"In Cama hospital, in Bombay, the incidence of girls delivering by caesarian section surgery was so much more than here. Is it that the girls in Mumbai are softer, and can't bear the rigours of labour, and want the easier approach?"

"Maybe the city girls have to take a lesson or two from their Adivasi counterparts."

"Dadan, don't say this in Bombay. The girls won't like it."

....And we were all laughing at the thought of Dadan being scalped by the women in Bombay.

35. A Touching Moment

It was the festive season of nine nights, Navratri. And tomorrow was the last day, the culmination of nine nights of revelry.... Dassehra. This festival is celebrated across India with due pomp and splendour. It is the festival that celebrates the victory of good over evil. But....There were no major celebrations in Jawhar. In Jawhar it was life as usual except with the townspeople, who wore their new fineries and exchanged sweets. In Jawhar, there was no song and dance as is seen in Bombay.

Hiroo was going home to be with his family, Yogendra, Hemant and Sayed were planning to come in the course of the next two weeks. We were going to see a major reshuffle in the hospital in a week's time.

Dadan and I took off for rounds, whilst Hiroo prepared to leave. He was going to catch the 11am bus.

Our first stop was at the maternity ward to check on the three deliveries done this morning. All of them were well and the babies were delightful. All three families had arrived and there was an atmosphere of joy prevailing in the maternity ward. The nurses had imparted the instructions about breast feeding and care of the breasts to all the mothers. We decided to keep them in hospital for one day in order to allow time for the mothers to 'room-in' adequately.

Dhavali was next on the list. On the whole she was a lot better but, today she was restless and, obviously, missing her husband. Yesterday's deliveries and the ensuing joy must have undoubtedly opened a few wounds in her heart as she looked melancholy today. Understandably so. I made a mental note of coming back to her after my work to have a heart to heart talk with her. That would need a lot of time. I knew that if I were to get to the root of her problems, and to trace the events that lead to her being in this state, it would be akin to wading through a rainforest. I should prepare to face torrential rain, figuratively speaking. If I wanted to see her well again I would have to get there.

Potya was fine. His stitches were remarkably clean and he was hungry. He had had his breakfast and was now walking about in the corridor. His course of antibiotics and Mebendazole were almost over. We could consider discharging him in a day or two, though he was keen to leave right away. We all agreed it would be more prudent for him to stay for a day or two longer.

In the female ward, Laxmi and her husband were waiting for me. Her bleeding had completely stopped after receiving 250cc of ASV.

The blotches on the skin, mute testimony of her recent ordeal, were already fading. She was much better now. Her husband asked me tentatively if he could take her home. I thought for a while.

There was no reason to keep her in the hospital. It was apparent that the worst was over and the rest of the recovery could very well be made at home. With these considerations I consented to discharge her in the afternoon.

"Doctor, there is a bus at 12 that takes us to our village. After that there is no bus till 6 in the evening. Can you help me catch the bus at noon?"

I was suddenly reminded of the fact that he had brought Laxmi on foot, on that terrible night, with his brother's help, and hence, this time, he wanted to reach home safely before dark.

"Okay, I'll make your papers now. You will then be able to catch the bus at 12." After finishing my rounds in the female ward I headed straight for the nursing station to prepare Laxmi's discharge papers and finish the paper work. I kept her on a host of vitamin supplements and stopped everything else. I asked the nurse to explain the details of the treatment at home to Laxmi, after which they could leave if they wanted.

Dadan had finished most of the OPD cases. The remaining few were being seen together by us when the nurse came in and informed us that Laxmi was ready to leave and that her husband wished to meet us. "Send him in, Sister."

He came in and indicated with a broad smile that they were ready to leave. I expressed my best wishes to him.

"I wanted to say something to you...."he said tentatively. He came in closer and then slowly, thoughtfully, he squatted on the floor on his haunches. He had a sheepish, embarrassed, hesitant look on his face. The look on his face was difficult to describe. He spoke nothing but his expression conveyed, at that moment, a thousand different emotions. It was a look that said everything. He didn't speak for a moment as if to gather his thoughts. Then he said," Doctor,....you have saved my Laxmi's life. I have no words to thank all of you." His words of gratitude, and the way he said them, touched me to the core of my heart and I was at a complete loss for words. I just kept looking at him. His face, wizened by the vicissitudes of time, rugged beyond his real age, was a study of a million emotions all at once.

He didn't meet our eyes, but continued to say, "Doctor, I am a poor man and don't have anything to give to you. Yet..."he paused, and, taking his soiled and much used towel from his shoulder, untied a corner which had been knotted tightly. Having untied the knot, he slowly and deliberately extricated a crumpled, soiled, one rupee note. He unfolded it, patting the creases away, and then said, "Doctor, I can't leave without saying thank you. I want you to accept this small gift from me. Your help meant so much to me." He placed the rupee note on the table in front of me gently, dabbed his eyes with the towel on his shoulder, got up and left.

I was speech less....and battling my own emotions as they welled up. I just couldn't react. His gesture had stormed my senses. In what felt like an eternity, I scrambled back to reality and got up to go after him. We were slow to react, and as we got to the front porch of the hospital, we saw Laxmi and her husband already walking down the hill, at quite a distance from us. I wanted to call out, but there was no voice. We were both overwhelmed. We just watched as the couple rounded the next bend and disappeared. I looked at the note in my hand for a long, hard moment. This note meant the world to me. It was not currency,....it was pure, unadulterated love and gratitude.

Laxmi's husband had left a profound impact on our minds. His simple deed had touched us so deeply. Dadan and I had discussed this at lunch, and had expressed so many thoughts on how life in Bombay was, and how different it was in this remote village. The values, the respect, the modes of expression.... everything was so different. In Bombay when you did something good for someone they thanked you and left. If they were well-to-do, you would get a gift of some sweets or some object or a card. That was the gratitude we were used to. What we had seen this morning was something extraordinary, something that swept us off our feet, caught us completely unawares. For a man to whom every rupee matters, a gift of one rupee could spell the difference between going home by bus or going home on foot. His sincere gratitude, and method of expressing it, had touched our hearts so deeply that, at present, it defied description.

36. An Unexpected Invitation

Being the season of festivals, the attendance at the hospital had nearly halved and there were few patients in the clinic and there would be fewer admissions to the wards. The respite was always welcome. The time of rest is the time to sharpen the weapons as the saying goes.

At about 5pm we received a call from Dr. Nisal.

"Let's go and see what he wants."

We found him still in his office, or chamber, as he liked to call it. He was sipping on some tea and seemed to be in an unusually affable mood. He bid us come in. "Gokani, Dadan, what is your programme tomorrow? Are you boys doing something?"

I looked at Dadan and seeing his quizzical look, I gathered what he must be thinking. Maybe Dr. Nisal wants to give us a party. I think we were both on the same wavelength.

"We have no plans, Sir. It's just the two of us presently, and actually, we had not even thought of doing anything tomorrow."

"Why? Where are the others?"

"Sir, they had to attend family functions so they have gone home. Three of them will come back in a day or two."

"I was thinking we would do something in the hospital tomorrow. It's Dassehra and it's an auspicious day. We should do something."

"What did you have in mind, Sir?"

"Come home for dinner. Tomorrow 8 o'clock."

Sir, thank you so much. But, Sir.... it would be too much trouble for Ma'am. We'll come for tea, Sir."

"No trouble, boys. Dinner. We will all eat together. I've called Ujwala and Dhande also."

Secretly we thought....Wow! He's calling us for dinner. Maybe a feast. Why should we let it go!

"Okay, Sir. We will be there." So saying, we slipped out of his room. This was a surprise! To be invited by the CMO for dinner?

Something that never happened before. We were excited and amused.

Once we were out of earshot, we looked at each other and burst into laughter.

"So? We have a feast tomorrow? He is benevolent! We must have done something good. He called us 'boys'! Boys! That was warm."

"I think he likes us. I don't think he called anyone home in the past. He brings sweets to the office ...but never called us home.... That too, for dinner!"

"Good, so our Dassehra is taken care of."

"Yes!"

"We better tell Vahini about this."

"Vahini? O Vahini!" We called out as we approached her room.

"What is it?" she said a tad tritely.

"Vahini, good news for you! Tomorrow you don't have to cook dinner for us."

"You have a free day after tea."

"What free day!? There's never a free day for me." She was sulking.

"Why, Vahini?" In mock sympathy.

"What's the matter, Vahini? Why do you look upset?" Still teasing her.

"You say free day? Do you know something? You have all been invited to the CMO's home for dinner......and do you know who is going to cook? I have to cook! Madame asked me to cook for six people tomorrow. And I was so looking forward to the respite of having to cook only for the two of you. Now instead of two, I have to cook for six!"

"Oh, no! That's a tough one, Vahini. We thought Madame would be cooking. So tomorrow your Dassehra is sunk!"

"Yes."

"So, Vahini, tell me. What are you going to cook tomorrow? Is it the same stuff you cook for us everyday?" I was teasing her too much. We knew she was annoyed at the prospect of having to work double time on a big holiday. "Are you going to cook something tasty tomorrow?"

"Stop it, Anand! Why are you teasing her? She is already upset and you are not doing anything to ease her situation."

"Okay, okay! Sorry, Vahini, sorry!"

This hasty apology made her break into her signature smile. Looking at us, she said, "Normally I love my holidays, and don't like all this extra work. It's because of you that I said yes. Is there anything you would like me to make?"

I set off again,"Vahini, make Shrikhand-puri, aloo tikis, biryani, chholé....!"

"Shut up, Anand!!" Dadhan said. "You are making fun of her. Poor lady! Vahini, don't listen to him. He is just being mean."

Vahini was still smiling her broad, good-natured smile. She actually loved cooking for us. She would cook and we would eat and she would listen to our prattle about life, patients, colleagues, the hospital, and everyone and everything under the sun.

We were sure now that we were really in for a feast tomorrow.

With thoughts of tomorrow's dinner we settled for tonight's simple fare. Dreams of good food plagued hungry, homesick interns all night long. There were no calls. The night was peaceful, save for the beating of drums to a primeval rhythm, far in the distance.

Some Adivasis were ushering in Dassehra this year. Even the crickets seemed to be lying low today.

37. A Visitor!

At the crack of dawn, as the first rays of the rising sun pierced the morning mist, there was a knock on the door. This knock was not the knock calling us to see a patient. It was different. The knock from Mukne, the watchman, was a firm, confident and familiar one. It brought you out of bed with a start. This was a soft, tentative knock. It was surely someone not accustomed to knocking on our door. I opened the door and looked out.

"Arrey tumhi!" it was our farmer friend who supplied us with milk. "Namaste! How are you? Come in. Come in." Calling out to Dadan, I said,"Arrey, Dadan, see who is here. Krishna bhau."

Dadan hurriedly got out of bed and came to the door. "Come in. Come in. What a pleasant surprise."

Krishna bhau came in and sat himself on a chair in the anteroom. He placed a package on the table and said,"I came to wish you a Happy Dassehra. I thought I'd start by visiting you and then meet the others. You have been doing so much good work in the hospital and we have seen how much goodwill you have earned in these few months.

"Today I have brought for you some sweets, made at home, for you to enjoy. This is our way of saying that we really appreciate your presence amongst us. There is not a single household in the town that has not spoken well of you all. These sweets are not just from me, they are a token of gratitude from the townspeople.

"Thank you doctors, for being a friend and doctor for us." He spoke these words with the deepest sincerity. His feelings came across to touch our hearts.

Krishna bhau was always our well-wisher. He hardly met us but he sent us that half litre of milk every day without fail. He had also spared milk for Dhavali's babies when they were alive. He had never asked for anything in return and was a man of few words. He expressed better with his deeds and acts of kindness. Apparently he observed us from near and from far. He had lived in Jawhar all his life and knew almost everyone that mattered. So anything that happened in town rarely escaped his notice.

Hospital news travelled like wild fire, the good and the bad. The main purveyors of gossip, or news if I may say so, were Haribhau, Vahini, Maushi, Vashani, Mukne and the sisters. Our adventures, and misadventures, in the wards, were the topics of hot gossip.

Through them, news spread. Vahini had not arrived as yet, hence we couldn't offer Krishna bhau any tea.

We expressed our deepest gratitude to him and sought his blessings in return.

"Krishna bhau, it was so nice of you to bring us sweets. Your gesture is heart- warming. We are touched. We feel a oneness with all of you, and not like outsiders. We are beginners and want to do good for people, and learn at the same time. Your good wishes and encouragement have strengthened our desire to do well and work hard."

"Happy Dassehra!" Dadan and I wished him in unison.

"Dassehra Mubarak!" We shook hands with him and exchanged warm hugs.

"Thank you, Krishna bhau." He bid us farewell and left with the promise of meeting again. No sooner he left, we opened the box of sweets and delved into it...greedily... No! Enthusiastically! It was a super beginning to an auspicious day.

Vahini made breakfast for us whilst we got ready for the day.

"Vahini, what's for breakfast today?" I asked, peeping into the kitchen. On seeing her stirring the contents in the vessel I exclaimed,"Seera!! Wow ! Dadan, seera !"

"I know," he said with a broad smile on his face, "Your favourite! Fill your stomach with it."

"I'm going easy. It's just too good. But we have plenty of food coming for us today"

"When we started the day with Krishna bhau's sweets the rest of the day would be packed with sweets!"

38. Tara

After breakfast we set off to take rounds. Today the clinic was closed on account of the holiday. Just as well. That gave us more time to take a leisurely and thorough ward round. We started the rounds from the maternity ward. The three deliveries done two days back were all doing well. The mothers were in good shape. The two baby boys were doing well, cherubic, thrashing their limbs with abandon, suckling well and a joy to behold. They seemed ready to go home.

"Would you like to go home?" we asked the two mothers and their faces lit up.

"Yes, please!"

"Okay, I'll prepare your discharge papers after my ward rounds. All the best." Before parting, we gave one last affectionate tweak to the boys' cheeks and then moved on to the next cot.

It was the baby girl born to her mother after induction of labour with the help of Pitocin. The mother was doing well. She was smiling and all set to leave, heartened by the fact that the earlier mothers' and their babies were being sent home today. Her baby.......

"Dadan, does she look yellow? A bit more than usual?" So saying, I picked up the infant and walked out of the ward to where the sunshine was direct. I couldn't really tell the colour of the baby's skin in the diffuse light inside the ward. Out in the broad daylight, the baby looked yellow, more than usual. The mother had followed me out of the ward and we were standing in the open yard outside the maternity ward. The broad smile on the mother's face was replaced by a furrow on her brow. A tinge of anxiety crept into her voice as she realised that something was amiss. Something that was worrying her doctors. Everything else was fine. The child was suckling well, all her reflexes were normal, and her vital signs were all within normal limits. She was just a tinge more yellow than I expected. The causes of neonatal jaundice clicked away in my mind.....infection? ....doesn't look like it... Drugs?..... Umm....Other causes?...... We went over the child again, more carefully this time.

The heart, the lungs, the abdomen, the nervous system, the skin .....all normal. No sign of any infection. Yet, she was yellow!

Okay, we will figure out the cause later. Currently what do we do? Observe her carefully. Do we use any medications, any procedures, anything that may help the baby stay normal. My mind was working feverishly to find answers to a hundred questions. In the city, during our urban posting, we had seen several cases of neonatal jaundice. Visions of kernicterus, neurological problems, exchange transfusions,......drugs?....Drugs!!?... Yes, of course, could this be a side effect of Pitocin, used during labour? Who could we ask?

"Dadan, do you think that Pitocin used during delivery can cause an exaggeration of physiological jaundice in the baby?"

"I'm not sure, yaar. Maybe."

"What shall we do for the baby?"

"She is fine presently. Let's not panic."

We turned to the mother who had anxiety writ large on her pretty face. She looked like she was going to cry. I said to her, "Don't worry. The child is normal. Just a bit yellow. We would like to watch her for a day or two."

"What is wrong with her?" she asked anxiously,"Please tell me."

"Tai, there is nothing wrong with your baby. Every baby, after birth, turns yellow after it is two or three days old and becomes normal after a week. This jaundice is normal in healthy children. In some cases though, the jaundice is more than usual and for those babies we have to do certain things. Presently, your baby is perfect but we want to watch her carefully so that she doesn't get any problem later. Don't worry."

My words didn't take the furrow off her brow, though she did resign herself to stay on. The baby in her arms, nestled comfortably, was oblivious of her mother's concerns.

"Tai, give her your milk as often as she demands, you drink lots of fluids, and eat well. When the sun is soft and mild, keep the baby in the sun. Sit in the sun with her on your lap and the sunshine will help reduce the yellowness." The yard just outside of the maternity ward was an open space and the sunshine there was just right for the mother and baby to bask in. I asked her to sit down at the edge of the paving with her legs stretched out and place the baby on the outstretched legs and stay there till it was too warm to endure.

"Keep the sun out of the baby's eyes," I cautioned. "Put a white handkerchief on the child's eyes and head."

She settled down on the floor as instructed. "Tai, don't worry at all. It's nothing serious. It is normal to be yellow at this point in time, but since your baby is a bit more yellow than normal, we are taking these precautions. In two days she will be back to her normal colour.... and she will be the prettiest little girl ever!"

She smiled a wry smile. Not fully convinced, but getting there slowly.

"Have you thought of a name? What are you going to call her?"

"We haven't decided yet. My husband's sister will decide the name. That is the custom."

"Can we suggest a name for her? Call her.... Tara."

"Yes. Tara meaning star! She is a Star!"

She was now smiling broadly, with the anxiety wiped off her face. We left her sitting in the morning sunshine, with the thought of a nice name for her child. And Tara, oblivious of her malady, was busy thrashing her limbs and gurgling in her own special language which only her mother understood.

39. I Want to Go Home!

The next patient was Potya. He was much better and was digesting his food well, had gained in strength and was fully ambulatory. He smiled as he saw us, and the first thing he uttered, no sooner we reached his bed was," I want to go home, please."

"Wait a minute. Let me examine you." I said. His vital signs were normal and his abdomen was soft. Everything looked good, save the fact that his stitches were still in place, and would be removed only on the fourteenth day after surgery. If he went home, who would remove the sutures? What if he developed an infection after going home? Our city-bred thinking was looking to the optimum scenario.

"Doctor, you have saved my life. Now I am fine. Let me go. It's Dassehra and I want to be home with my family, please."

"Potya, if you go home who will remove the stitches? Will you come back to have your stitches removed after a week?"

"I can only come back after a month. We live far from here and the bus stop is very far. We are deep in the interiors."

"One month! No! It's too long. Is there any doctor nearby?.... or a nurse?... or any medical facility?"

"There is an animal doctor there. He lives about three miles from where we are. Would he be able to remove the stitches?"

"You mean a proper animal doctor with a degree?" The direction this conversation was taking was leaving us aghast. We were finally coming to terms with a veterinary doctor removing Potya's sutures in the village. Visions of Potya being take to the cow barn to see this doctor who wore overalls, and was grimy from head to toe .... And my imagination ran amok. I shook off the reverie and returned to reality. Did I have a choice?

"Yes. We think he has a degree from Nashik. He treats our cows and buffaloes and sometimes the dogs ...he gives them injections ....and ..."

"and sometimes he treats human beings also!" I completed his sentence for him. We were all laughing now, more from the irony of it all than from the actual humour. The ways of the village were beyond anyone's comprehension. by a long shot. "Okay, I'll write you a letter for him explaining what he should do for you. You can go and have your stitches cut by him. And. in case he is not available or if you have any problems, you can come back to us."

It did take a short while to reconcile that the world of the village was very different from the urban system we lived in and subscribed to. The law of the jungle was so different, that it challenged the imagination to comprehend the logic or the philosophy.

His papers were prepared and he left a very happy man. His farewell was a touching moment. More than ten of his family members and friends had come to take him home. They mobbed our little nursing station to thank us and say goodbye. It was a touching sight to see him go, happy....and in one piece. It was a week ago when we had made our adventurous and daring decision to operate on him. I shuddered even as I thought of all that could have gone wrong. The vision of the bloated intestines lying on the towel drapes on the surgical table, outside of the abdomen, and the vivid vision of the intestine turning black with the application of the Babcock's forceps, made me shudder again. The sound of our united gasp and the call to immediately remove the forceps rung loud in my ears even after so many days. The sight of Potya leaning over the ledge and retching violently, the worms wriggling on the floor, in his nostril and his mouth, sent a shiver down my spine again, Thank God he is better! that was all I could think of, as he walked away. It was anybody's guess when we would meet again..... Or whether we would meet again, ever!

40. Tara's Medicine

The rounds were over and now we had to return for the Dassehra puja at 6 pm. We were free till then. On our way back to the room we stopped by at Vashani's door.

"Vashani-ji. Have you got the phenobarbitone tablets?"

"Yes! Yes! I got them two days back."

Oh! That's great! Dadan, Do you think we can give that girl's baby.....Tara ...phenobarb for the jaundice?"

"Never used it, yaar. Do you know the dose?"

"Oh no! I'm not sure of the dose in infants!"

"ANAND!! Neonatal jaundice happens only in infants...not in adults, yaar!"

Dadan, was being mischievously deprecating. Scoffing at my incomplete theoretical knowledge. But I was not to be cowed down, "Vashani-ji, one tablet is 30mg, isn't it?"

"Yes it is," he said, peering at the packet in his hand.

"Make four pieces of one tablet and give me eight such pieces. I want them in the next half an hour. I'm giving the kid 7.5 mg twice a day and will watch her. Let's see what happens. Won't do any harm, I think." I said, turning to Dadan as we moved away from the pharmacist.

"Your call, Anand. I don't know this treatment."

It's given in Nelson and in Goodman-Gilman,. Can't be wrong then. I'm giving it." The arrogance and the daring of the young and inexperienced being amply demonstrated in this pattern of behaviour. A trait that dies with the passage of Time and the attainment of some Wisdom. As the saying goes....Fools rush in, where Angels fear to tread. Whither wisdom! The maverick exhibits daring and adventure!

After a short period of reflection Dadan spoke again,"Anand, phenobarb is a hypnotic, no?"

"Yes, it is. So?"

"Suppose the bachchu becomes drowsy with your phenobarb experiment, then?"

Trust Dadan to throw a googly when you least expect it. "Hey, that's a possibility."

"Then....How will we distinguish between the bilirubin reaching the brain versus the side effect of the drug. How will we know the difference?"

"Point, yaar! Tu really bahut sochta hai! You really think too much."

"What will we do if that happens?......Idea! We'll give the mother two cups of coffee everyday?"

Now it was my turn to be nonplussed, "Pray, how will that work, my friend?"

Dadan replied with a smile, having gained a victory over me, he said,"Arrey, elementary, Anand! We give the phenobarb to the baby, she becomes drowsy. We give the coffee to the mother, the caffeine from the mother's blood comes in the milk, the baby drinks the breast milk, the caffeine goes in her blood and wakes her up!" Dadan ended with a triumphant thump on the table.

"WAH, DADAN, WAH!!!! You are a genius!" His theory was technically unassailable."You go and tell the girl yourself...and also take some coffee for her. She won't be having any of her own." I was smiling uncontrollably with Dadan's spontaneous and original theory.

But,...it wasn't in vain. The little girl, Tara, as we had already christened her, showed remarkable improvement in the next three days. Simply sun exposure, breast milk and phenobarb, and her skin had the radiant pink hue with all traces of yellow gone by the third day. Seeing her get better was an enormously uplifting experience. Those rare occasions when you can use advanced knowledge which was acquired, much against mainstream advice, at some time late in the night, from an advanced book, not recommended for the course. It was a moment of truth, a re- affirmation of the tenet that knowledge must be accumulated painstakingly, putting aside personal comforts because, you never know when it will be of use to someone lost in the darkness of ignorance and suffering. That experience with phenobarbitone and the outcome being Tara's recovery was testimony to this fact.

41. The Pooja!

It was about 5pm when we realised that we need to start getting ready to reach the clinic.

"Hey! One problem."

"What problem.?"

"No new clothes, yaar. Everyone will be dressed in new clothes and we will be in our rags."

"Who cares, yaar. Don't worry about the townspeople and the staff. Look at the Adivasis. Do they have new clothes? Do they even have clothes?

Silence.

"Then why worry? What we are. we are! New or old, clothes don't make us better or worse. It's who we are that matters. Isn't it?"

"True. Well said. Likh daal!!! Write it down !!" On that immensely philosophical note we decided that we didn't need to really dress up for the occasion.

At 6 pm Dadan and I made our way to the clinic. Everyone was already there. The nurses looked beautiful in their gorgeous colourful sarees, the ward boys, Haribhau and Vahini, Vashani, Dr. Dhande and Dr. Nisal. Like one large family we had gathered. The girls had decorated an image of Goddess Mahalaxmi with flowers, fruit, incense sticks, and a diya with pure ghee was placed in front of the Goddess' image. On another table were the instruments that we use every day, a stethoscope, a percussion hammer, a torch and a blood pressure measuring instrument. These were symbolic of the tools of our trade. It was an interesting mix of objects on the table and so also an interesting mix of people in the room.

Dr. Nisal made his way closer to the corner of worship and, pulling a match box from his pocket, lit the diya and the incense sticks. The fragrance of the incense and the ghee soon pervaded the air in the room. An expectant hush prevailed in the room as everyone was keenly awaiting the next move. Dr. Nisal then asked if anyone could chant some shlokas or mantras. Everyone in the room smiled sheepishly, looking at one another, hoping someone would take the lead.

"Come on! Someone has to say the prayers. Who will do it? Speak up."

The girls looked hesitant, self-conscious and shy. Left to themselves they were unstoppable in speech but it was at such moments that they reverted to their protective shells and clammed up.

"Anand, you?"

"Sir, I'm not good at rituals but I can say the GAYATRI mantra. Is that okay?"

"Yes! Yes! That's good. I know that rituals are difficult and, at times, meaningless for us. It's the spiritual part that is important. The faith and belief. It is faith alone that helps us through any difficult time. So go ahead, Anand."

A bit hesitant, a bit self-conscious, tentative and nervous, lest I forget the mantra midway, I started.

"AUM BHUR BHUVASWAHA, TATSAVITUR VARENYAM, BHARGODEVASYA DHEEMAHI, DHEYO YONAH PRACHODAYAT."

Those gathered in the room repeated this mantra with me three times. "This Mantra is an earnest plea to the All Pervading, Omniscient, Omnipresent Almighty to grant us the wisdom and skill to always pursue the Right Path."

"On this Dassehra day, we will all resolve to continue working like a team and doing the work as we have been doing always. Sisters, please do the Arti." For this they needed no goading.

They sang the entire Arti whilst illuminating the image of Goddess Mahalaxmi with the lamp of ghee. Everyone joined in with the singing, lending the office a new found spiritual charm. After the Arti, sweets were offered and greetings exchanged. In about half an hour, the customary ritual was over. There were broad smiles all around.

The nurses and Vahini had taken great pains to dress up and look beautiful. They looked every bit fit for the occasion. Their efforts, undoubtedly, added grace and charm to the occasion. Their rendition of the Arti was also perfect. The entire ritual had brought us all together and the camaraderie was palpably warm.

Vahini left shortly after the pleasantries had been exchanged, whilst the nurses and the other staff lingered, engaged in light conversation and laughter. The atmosphere at the hospital had, for once, taken on a light-hearted hue. We sat around with the nurses, chatting and sharing some frivolous banter with them. Normally, it would be serious talk, exchanging information about patients, or giving orders for their treatment, or sometimes, just sharing moments in silence, giving each other the unspoken encouragement that strengthens the bond that exists between nurses and doctors.

Today there was mirth and merriment. Stories of the past, our idiosyncrasies, our follies and foibles, all surfaced and were greeted with peals of laughter. Nobody was spared. The nurses who worked silently, never missed anything. They watched us closely, and today, they unabashedly exposed our habits and weaknesses. Ruthlessly, almost vengefully. But all this in the spirit of love and bonhomie. Only at these moments does one realise how these silent, docile and obedient nurses imbibe everything that they see, and when your guard is down, they bring it all out. Mimicry, anecdotes, idiosyncratic behaviour, and anything else that distinguishes you from the rest. They knew it all and now they were having a field day at our expense. Time flew and soon it was 8 pm. Time for dinner at the boss' home!

42. The Dinner

"It's eight."

"Let's go. We better be on time."

"Anand....? We are going empty-handed. Is it okay?" queried Dadan. "Should have taken something, don't you think?"

"You are right, yaar! Now what? Is there anything we can take for them?"

"Nothing, yaar. Forget it! We'll get something for him next time. Anyway, in this village what can we get for them that they don't already have."

We walked up the flight of stairs to his residence and rang the doorbell. Within moments Mrs. Nisal opened the door, "Welcome, welcome! Please come in!" Her warmth was instantly disarming. It was like being welcomed home after being away for months. If we had any qualms about having dinner with the boss, they were instantly dispelled. "Thank you Ma'am. Thank you for having us over."

She smiled affably and said,"Oh, come on ! This is just like your home. I've been wanting to meet you all since a long time. I thought this would be a good opportunity. I'm glad it all worked out."

"Yes, Ma'am."

Right behind Ma'am was Dr. Nisal. As we entered, he gave us a warm smile and a thump on the back. He was beaming, happy that we were all together. It was heart warming to be accorded such a warm and loving welcome.

Ujwala Narde had already arrived. "Hello Ma'am," we greeted her, "You look so charming in a saree." The compliment was sincerely meant 'cause she really looked pretty. We, indeed, had the devious propensity to tease her often, but this once, the compliment was heartfelt. She was smiling from ear to ear on receiving the compliments.

Dr. Ujwala had a fair complexion, with slight buck teeth and very good skin. Her eyes were hazel brown and her hair curly and black. Invariably, a few strands of hair at the forehead had a mind of their own and would escape the inadequate clip placed to keep them steady. She had a tic which we had noticed very early in our acquaintance and it always made us smile. She would smile coyly with a display of teeth and, every once in a while, she would have to push back strands of hair, which kept breaking loose and obstructing her vision. She would do this at a striking rate of three to four times a minute. Once we were aware of this we couldn't help following the strands wherever they went and smile at the repeated acts of disciplining them. It was these mannerisms and many more that she possessed, that endeared her to whoever met her or worked with her.

Just as we were about to sit down, the doorbell rang. "I'll get it," Dadan said, and got up to open the door. It was Dr. Dhande, looking immaculate as usual.

"Good evening, Sir."

"Good evening." he replied, greeting everyone with a broad smile.

"Come on in. we were waiting for you," said Mrs. Nisal, as she brought out some fruit juice as an appetiser with peanuts and chivda as accompaniments. I stole a glance towards the kitchen and caught sight of Vahini standing by the stove and cooking something in a large vessel.

"Namaskar, Vahini." I called out. She looked in my direction and her face lit up with a broad smile. In an instant she knew what I was thinking. Still smiling broadly, she returned her attention to the vessel on the stove, not wanting to burn or spoil her main dish for the evening.

This evening's get-together was a first of a kind. It was rare to be dining with the CMO or AMO as there was an hierarchy which precluded this closeness. Bosses kept a distance from the students and interns and the fine veil of authority kept the students away from their bosses. Today was different and I dare say that both sides knew it, and were having their problems breaking the ice.

Finally, Dr. Nisal broke the silence and started the conversation by saying," You know, that patient Dhavali, the one with the twins? I can't remember having done a surgery like that at this hospital ever in the past. I am still amazed at how you boys had the courage to undertake such a risky procedure. Generally such cases would have gone to Thane Civil."

Thane Civil Hospital was the referral hospital for the district and was equipped with expertise to handle such cases. However, getting there in such a situation was arduous and daunting to the poor village folk. It was expensive to travel the distance and the big city was too imposing for these simple, sheltered people.

"Sir, it would have been impossible without your support and encouragement. Our enthusiasm is not backed by experience. Your support gave us wings."

"Whatever the reasons, I must say that, given the circumstance, you boys have done a marvellous job with her. I am really proud of you all. Even the snake bite case, the cases of fever, dysentary, and the intestinal obstruction case...all well done."

"Thanks, Sir!" We were delighted with the effusive praise and were a tad embarrassed too, as we didn't know how to respond to this shower of appreciation.

After these opening remarks, he suddenly turned to me and asked,"Anand, aren't you planning to go home for a while? Your friends have all taken their breaks."

"Sir, I have overstepped my leave already. Now I can't afford any more leave. If I go now, you won't give me my completion certificate." I said with a tongue-in-cheek expression on my face. I was so keen to know how he would react to my last statement.

"No. No, Anand. You have worked diligently. Go for a few days if you like," he said. "I would be mean to deny you some respite."

"Oh, thank you so much, Sir! I'll adjust some leave with my colleagues around Divali. Thank you so much!"

The conversation in the room was centred around our college life and our families. Dr. Nisal wanted to know about our home, families, and our personal ambitions. The conversation continued and the evening warmed up. The juice, peanuts and chivda were running out. it is well known that interns on their rural posting are always hungry and are on a constant SEE FOOD diet. He will eat whenever he sees food. Greedy! Uncouth! Uncultured! And most certainly un-becoming of a physician in the making. Nevertheless, all considerations set aside, all inhibitions abandoned, and all caution thrown to the winds....every young doctor who goes through the rigours of physical, mental and spiritual hardship, realises that moments of happiness have to be grabbed, have to be cherished and have to be exploited to the fullest. Food is no exception!

"Dinner is ready," Mrs. Nisal called out to us. Having made short work of the juice and snacks laid out, we were ready for the big stuff. Dadan was first to get up. He was very keen to see what Vahini had made for dinner. Without being too obtrusive, he wandered off towards the dinner table to see what was being placed there. In a few moments we had all joined him. No sooner the food was laid out we all started to help ourselves.

Mrs. Nisal announced, "There is vegetable biryani, kadhi, bhindi, salad and parathas. Please enjoy the meal."

"Thank you Ma'am. Everything looks delicious."

The vegetable biryani smelled delicious, and looked good too. The kadhi went with the biryani topped with diced cucumber, onions, and tomato salad dressed with lemon juice. The paratha and bhindi were the side dishes. This was delicious fare and Dadan and I filled our plates and settled down to eat. We wanted to savour the food to the fullest. At this moment conversation was both irrelevant and unnecessary. Sit quietly and eat deliberately is an important adage for all. And that's exactly what we did.

Dr. Ujwala and Dr. Dhande were discussing something. Ma'am and Dr. Nisal were talking to Vahini appreciating her food, whilst Dadan and I were lost to the world. After nearly a month we were deriving devious pleasure in eating. Dadan whispered," I wish this was mutton biryani! It would have been the best ever!"

"Greedy! Dadan, be thankful for this much!" I whispered back.

"Dreaming doesn't invite tax! Man lives on hope!"

"Ya, that's true," I condescended.

The food was delicious and it was evident that Vahini had truly outdone herself today. Maybe it was to please us, or was it to please the boss! Don't really know. Who cares anyway. As long as we get good food.

"Ma'am, the food is outstanding. Really delicious. We are both stuffed."

"Ma'am. The biryani was really good. World class. As good as they make at home."

"Sudha is the true architect of this food. She deserves the credit. I only helped her a bit."

"Vahini! Nice food! Thank you!" She was beaming with pride and happiness with all this effusive praise. And she deserved every bit of all the praise and more, as she has worked all day to make our evening happy. Hard work, dedication, single-mindedness of purpose, diligence and the will to serve selflessly. That's our Vahini. Simple and loving. Always there to help. She doesn't just help, she does the entire job!

43. Politics in Medicine

The meal being done with, we drifted back to our original seats, Our discussion was veering towards the state of primary health care in Maharashtra and the shambles it was in.

"Ninety percent of the primary health care centres were being used as a base for private practice by the CMO and that's why he doesn't like interns. He perceives interns as a threat to the freedom to do private practice illegitimately. That's why the PHCs have gone to the dogs and the poor have no place to go."

"Why doesn't the government crack down on these corrupt practices. Are they party to this malpractice?"

"The government is well meaning but they don't have the wherewithal to crack down on a system that has mastered the art of corruption."

"It's really sad that the poor man has to suffer for no fault of his."

"Sir, what should be done to end these practices and catch the perpetrators?"

"Where will you start and whom will you catch. It's a stupendous task and, at every point, you will meet with opposition and obstacles. Presently, we can only do our work honestly and diligently and hope we can at least change the colour of the water to some extent. At least some of the people will get good medical care if we did our work as best as we could. At least you will know that your work has sent someone home happy and well. That's real happiness! The knowledge that someone felt good because you did something to ease their burden....is Happiness."

"It's really frustrating to see so much wrong-doing in this world and having to take all the bullshit lying down, and not being able to do anything about it. If it is left with the administration, they will never do anything about it. They have a thousand reasons ready to not do anything constructive or productive...."

"System! System! System!! Our whole damn system is defunct and derelict. We need to change at the grass-root level. We need to change the people around us. Who will do this for us?"

"Who will do it for you? You must do it alone......Ekla chalo re! Remember the Bengali song? Ekla chalo re....Walk alone! When you feel strongly enough, you will get to the bottom of the problem, weed it out, and destroy it. Mahatma Gandhi did it....Martin Luther King did it....and so many others in history did it. Go it alone and conquer your problems. As you go along, people will join you and the caravan will get longer and stronger."

Pause.

Long pause.

After this profound statement there was nothing more to say. Everyone was reflecting on what had just been said. It was eleven and time to leave.

I looked up to Mrs. Nisal and said,"Thank you for this lovely evening. Everything was marvellous. It felt like we were at home."

"Thank you for coming. Today your coming has brought so much life to our house. When it is just us, the house is so quiet. Please do come again."

"Yes Ma'am, we will come." So saying, we left to return to the quarters. It had been a long and adventurous day. Sleep beckoned.

44. In Ever-Widening Circles

It was dark, and the air was still. Not a breath of a breeze. I had been awake in bed for a while before I decided to take a walk to the dam. Dadan was fast asleep and was going to leave today for a week off from work. Hiroo, Yogendra and Hemant were supposed to return today.

The morning air was pleasant and had a fresh smell. The walk was exhilarating and the climate bracing. Coming up the street in front of me were a couple of villagers who must have been heading for their farms.

"Namaskar."

"Namaskar. Tumhi doctor sahib? Are you the doctor, Sir?"

"Ho. Yes. I am a doctor at the hospital."

"We guessed. Our friend was treated by you and he is very well now. He told us about you, the bearded doctor."

I couldn't help but smile. The beard sure made me famous, or at least easy to identify. This kind of recognition was good for a sagging ego. I was smiling for long after the farmers had passed me by. I was thinking to myself about how I had immersed myself in the work here so completely that I had not even written a letter home nor called. It had been a month since I left home and there had never been a dull moment.

"I better take a break as Dr. Nisal had suggested," I thought to myself. Maybe I should go back and get a little touch of the city before I become like the people that I treat. This thought had me smiling again.

The sun was making its first appearance by the time I reached the bend in the road that took me to the dam. The birds, too, had woken up and had got down to the business of feeding their young. A breathtaking atmosphere awaited me at the dam. The lake was still and beautiful. The glassy surface, unspoilt by ripples, reflected the opposite shore like a perfect mirror. There was not a soul at the dam. I found myself a place to sit and reflect on the myriad thoughts that plagued my mind. The peace at the lakeside was like balm to my tired mind. The soft hues of dawn, the chirping of the birds, and the soft rustling of the leaves were the music of a new morning.

Absently, I picked up a pebble and swung my arm to fling it over the lake. It soared high, arcing over to fall into the lake, somewhere in the middle, with a plop and splash.The 'plop' sound broke the silence and thereafter, a circular ripple broke the stillness of the glassy surface. Ripple after ripple, in ever-widening circles, spread rapidly across the surface of the lake. Soon to hit the shore, and gradually die out to return the lake to its original stillness.

My thoughts returned to the conversation that we had last night. Something about the system and its inherent defects. Where was the problem? Who was responsible for this decay. Is it that the administration is weak, ineffective?.... Was it that there was no accountability by the constituents of the system to the system? A complete lack of responsibility. When will the marginalised people stop being marginalised? When will there be a semblance of equality and an even distribution of resources? Did democracy not account for the poor?.... Or were they just vote banks, meant to be placated once in a while and then kept the way they were? Where does one start? And how does one move forward? Dr. Nisal was right. This was a very deep-seated problem and not for one person to tackle. Maybe we should just do what we are supposed to do and do it as well as we can do it. Maybe it would be only a drop in the ocean....but then....every drop made the ocean. Even a single effort, however small, would still make a difference. It would change the colour of the water.

I tossed another stone and watched the ripples form across the surface of the lake till they covered the entire lake. One stone can make a ripple, and that ripple makes another one, and another. and another. Till the lake is covered with ripples. One effort leads to a small result, that leads to another result, and gradually the effect spreads and continues to spread till it reaches everywhere. Thats it! That's how change occurs. With one Effort, by one Man, at one point in Time. I had my answer. We just had to continue what we were doing. Even if one centre worked optimally, it would take care of a section of people. However small the result, it would still be a result. And sooner or later, it would spread. How far this effect will travel? And for how long?....Only Time will tell!

45. Blunder and Regret!

The walk changed my mood and I was back to my optimistic self. When I returned to the room Dadan was getting ready to leave. We had breakfast together. Tea and upma. After Dadan left I would be alone till the others returned.

"When are you coming back?"

"One week or so? Anything you want from Bombay?"

"Nothing really. Can you phone my home and tell my mother that I am fine and that she should not worry. Tell her I will come sometime around Divali."

"You go in Divali. Syed and I will stay here and you guys can have your break and be with your families."

"I might just do that. I'll see. You have a nice trip."

"I will."

After bidding Dadan well, I left for the OPD. Today i would have to do the OPD by myself. The first patients had already arrived. I braced myself to face the first wave of diarrhoea, vomiting, fever, maybe some injuries, and anything else that chose to happen on that day. The OPD was uneventful except two patients.

There was this young man who had a very peculiar problem.... at least it looked peculiar till I understood its true meaning. He must have been about 20 years of age, otherwise in good health, presenting with multiple lumps on his ear, forehead, and other parts of his body. At first glance, I thought they must have been multiple sebaceous cysts. I asked him to see me after the OPD and I would see him more carefully.

The other patient, a 45-year-old, had presented with an ugly ulcer at the back of his ankle. I admitted him for wound care and daily dressings. He would need antibiotics and some regular food along with the wound care.

I finished my OPD at 2 pm. Tired and hungry, I headed for the nurses station to see if there were any other admissions made by the CMO or AMO. There were none. The young man with the 'multiple sebaceous cysts' was waiting for me at the nursing station.

I beckoned to him to come into the minor OT where I proceeded to examine him. The lumps on the face and ear looked exactly like sebaceous cysts to me. I thought I could excise one and see how it healed and then maybe, I could remove all of them for him. I made my first major mistake that day. I didn't carefully feel the lumps. I was so confident that they were exactly like sebaceous cysts and nothing else. In fact, I was OVER CONFIDENT!!! I called him to the minor OT at 3 pm. Allowing me enough time to grab a quick lunch. I had rounds to do, several dressings to be done, and there were some deliveries lined up for the night. There was much to be done today.

At 3 pm I headed for the minor OT. Sister Shinde was on duty. I asked her if she would assist me for a minor procedure. She consented, and after the paper work had been done, we took him and had him lie down on the operation table. I had planned on removing the lump on the ear. It looked really easy. One nick with a scalpel and a gentle squeeze to get the sticky material out and I would have proved my diagnosis and....I was about to launch on a misadventure I would regret.

After cleaning the part with spirit and iodine I infiltrated the ear with Xylocaine and, as soon as it had been rendered insensate, I took up the scalpel. "Keep the gauze ready, sister. As I make the nick, the discharge will ooze out. Please clean it with the gauze as it oozes."

"Yes, doctor."

I gripped the external ear firmly between my thumb and forefinger, and made the incision at the tip of the lump. There was a sudden gush of fresh blood as soon as I had done this. It caught me absolutely unawares. I was anticipating some cheesy, yellow material as is found in sebaceous cysts but instead, here was a gush of frank red blood! I was shocked for a second. In that moment his shirt and my hands were soaked in blood. This happened in the split second it took me to recover from my initial shock. "Sister! Quick! Artery forceps! Gauze! Quick sister! Fast! I grabbed the gauze in her hand and pressed it tightly against the ear at the point of bleeding. Within moments the gauze was soaked. The bleeding was rapid. Only too late, I realised that I was dealing with a vascular lump. an haemangioma!

I blindly clamped the external ear at the point of the incision, and yelled for sister to call Dr. Dhande, who was in his office next door. By the time he arrived, a few moments later, the bleeding had stopped, and I could see the cut edge, clamped by the artery forceps.

Dr. Dhande came over and was shocked to see the bloody mess! "What happened!"

"Sir, an error in judgement! My mistake, I was careless!" I said remorsefully. On seeing my crestfallen demeanour he softened and asked me to explain in more detail. "Sir, this patient came to the OPD this morning. I found him to be having several lumps on his face and body which I thought were sebaceous cysts. So I called him after OPD to excise one of them and confirm the diagnosis. I didn't palpate the lump carefully as I should have. No sooner I made the first incision I realised it's an haemangioma."

"Okay, let's put some stitches at the site of your incision and that will stop the bleeding. Then we will see what to do."

Sister had given him the suture material and he set about putting the sutures in place. Deftly, he stitched up the wound and when he was satisfied he unclamped the ear margin. No sooner he did that, there was bleeding from the incisional wound, despite the stitches. Dr. Dhande's face was a study in anxiety. He put a generous wad of cotton gauze on the wound and applied a tight sticking plaster and watched if the gauze was getting wet. It stayed the same.

Relief!

For the next ten minutes the gauze remained the same and showed no signs of further bleeding. We asked the patient to sit up. His shirt, neck and parts of his face were covered with his blood. The sight filled me with renewed remorse. Why did I do this? Why was I so careless?

I asked Sister to admit him and to keep him there till we were sure that the bleeding had stopped completely. After wiping him clean with a wet towel, Sister gave him a clean shirt from the hospital stock.

In an hour my upbeat mood had changed to severe regret and depression. I had caused so much undue pain and suffering to this patient just by being careless and overconfident. I realised that confidence built by days of hard labour and diligent study could come crashing down in a moment of carelessness. This was, without an iota of doubt, my worst moment.

After reassuring the patient and explaining to him the nature of the problem, I returned to the room to' lick my wounds' so to speak. I was severely shaken and regretful. I had not imagined that I could drop my guard so totally and so comprehensively. Was it my pride and youthful cockiness that lead to this unceremonious fall?

Careless? Callous?. Careless, yes! Callous, not quite! I had no intention to do this. It was a sheer accident that happened in my unguarded moments.

I brooded for the rest of the day, all by myself, in the room. My morale was shattered, my confidence was shaken and my equanimity disturbed. How will I retrieve what I had lost?

At 7pm I returned to the wards to take my rounds. I started with the maternity ward. One look at all the patients revealed that none of them were likely to deliver tonight.

Dhavali was at peace with herself. She was eating well now and her colour was returning. Though she was getting better, her mood was always pensive. We kept her busy with light activities to keep her from fretting. She did all the work and never seemed to mind, yet she never smiled.

How could she? She had lost two children in one week. She had made a superhuman effort to reach the hospital on that fateful monsoon night battling the rain, rough terrain, pain, weakness, swelling and the severe anxiety. She had reached us alive with only one motivation. That she could save the children. But that was not to be. How could she smile? Dhavali was battling a greater feeling of loss than I was. I needed to have that pending conversation with her, which I had pushed off for another day.

The other patients were fine. The man with the ulcer on the foot needed a dressing on the foot and medication. His wound had been neglected for far too long and hence had festered. Owing to the precarious location of the wound, at the back of the foot over the Achilles tendon, the wound was constantly breaking down. Walking around and the movements of the foot were breaking the wound as well. That foot needed to be immobilised. I needed to figure that out next.

And finally my last patient, the one I had caused so much anguish. He was asleep. I chose not to disturb him....or did I choose not to aggravate my own wounds. The wounds of severe regret and remorse. The wounds of anguish and repentance. I don't know which it was. I returned to the room....still in a melancholy mood.

46. Introspection in Solitude

Back in the room, I realised that I was alone at home for the first time since I had come to Jawhar. It was the solitude I needed to address my feelings frontally. I ate in silence, ruminating on the day's events and nursing a deep regret for my careless actions. My only option was to accept the mistake, to learn from it and to move on, more experienced. I consoled myself with the thought that everyone has his bad days and everyone makes mistakes. It's only the mistakes that we make and the lessons that we derive from them, that teach us to be better at what we do.

What pained me more was the fact that an innocent patient had to be the instrument for whatever profound lesson I had to learn, and that he had to suffer for my mistake. On reflecting on his treatment, I counted all the options possible in the management of his condition, and concluded finally that he would be best left alone. He had multiple haemangiomata and cutting them all would not be possible.

My mistake rankled me through dinner, but after I finished my mind was clearer and my thinking more organised, I decided to put this event behind me and approach the problem differently tomorrow morning. It would be best to talk to the patient up-front, re-assure him, and tell him all about the disease and all the treatment options. At the end of my rumination I came to two very important conclusions. Conclusions that would stay with me throughout my career as a physician.

The first lesson was: NEVER make an important decision on an empty stomach. You would be sure to either compromise safety or compromise a relationship by saying something rude or unsympathetic.

The second lesson was more profound: it was the fact that we were human beings,...doctors, we were not God and hence we must never entertain the delusion that we are. We must realise that, in spite of the best knowledge, best intentions, best resources, best teachings, and best support systems, we are prone to make mistakes, at times to the patients' detriment. We, as physicians should stop believing that we are infallible and that we can never make a mistake. Every human being, somewhere, sometime, reaches his level of incompetence and we must realise and remember this fact with full clarity. We must realise that we can make mistakes, we can be ignorant, we can forget, and we can misunderstand. If we realise these basic facts, we will actually be less prone to make mistakes. We will be more humble, and more open to suggestions which, in fact, may serve to improve the quality of our work.

This crystallised thought gave me immense solace. Having gone over the events of the day in minute and critical detail, and to have reached a profitable, logical, and beneficial solution, felt extremely gratifying. It was easier to deal with my grief now. I was relieved and reassured. With that good feeling I decided to call it a day.

47. Dhavali Wants to Go Home

The new day dawned bright and sunny, I had overslept. I was going at a relaxed pace since the holiday feeling still continued to prevail. Vahini made me some tea and breakfast which I ate deliberately, my mind planning the day step-by-step.The rounds were light. Dhavali's dressing had to be done and the patient with the foot ulcer needed a dressing.

When I reached the ward I was delighted to note that Dhavali's husband had returned. He looked extremely happy to be reunited with his wife. She was delighted too and, for once, she was actually smiling.

"How is everything at home?"

"Where do I begin, doctor? The story is so long and complicated," he said with a sigh.

"Tell me everything." I was, indeed, keen to know what had transpired in his village in his absence.

"Doctor, thank you for giving me the money to go by bus. I reached home in two hours after I left from here. On reaching, I discovered that someone had raided my farm and removed all the chillies that I had planted and which were now ready to be harvested.

"Did you find out who did that? Did you ask around?"

"I did find out. It was my neighbour and he said than since I wasn't there he thought of taking them lest they were wasted."

"Huh! Just because you were not there, he decided to plunder your farm. What kind of law is that. Did he give you the money he got by selling them?"

"He is not a bad man. He did it in good faith. He took some money for the labour he put in and gave me the rest. Actually, he never knew when I would return so he thought, better sell the chillies than waste them."

"Oh, that's okay then. Glad you got something. Now that you are back, I want to tell you about Dhavali's progress."

"She looks so much better now than when I left her four days ago. Thank you so much for looking after her so well. I didn't have to worry about her when I was away. I knew she was in good hands. I don't think I can match your care when I take her home."

"No, no! You look after her so well. We were marvelling, just the other day, at how you carried her from your home to the hospital in the dark of night and with such heavy rains." He flushed with the comment and smiled broadly.

"Coming back to the main point. I want to tell you that Dhavali has been getting better day by day and now her blood is more red, her swelling has gone and she is stronger. Her wound is also much better and cleaner, but will take some time to close. She is also a lot more cheerful now than she was earlier."

"Doctor, I want to take her home. There is a lot of work I have to do. If she is at home I can keep one eye on her and also keep an eye on my work. Once she is at home she will start feeling better. She will be happy at home. Please, doctor, let us go home."

I had never considered any option other than her going home only after full recovery, This was a new dimension that never crossed my mind. "No. You can't go!" My reflex, instinctive answer. His face fell when I said this with such finality. Frankly, I wasn't prepared to let her go till the wound on her abdomen had closed. She had suffered enough already. The thought of sending her home with a gaping wound was unthinkable.

He said nothing further but sat silently, watching as I did the dressing for Dhavali. My mind was weighing his request critically.

He had thrown in a new angle to the situation. What if the open wound got infected? What if she didn't get adequate nutrition and slipped back into a similar state? What if she had no help there?

More questions! No answers.

She looked a lot better now and was more communicative too. She re-iterated her husband's request,"Doctor, please. Let me go home. I will take care. Please let me go?"

Her beseeching looks softened my heart, forcing me to reconsider. After much vacillating in my mind, and weighing all the pros and cons, I decided to give her a month's stock of vitamins and protein powder and let her go. After all, one day she will have to go and care for her self. I couldn't make her so dependent on us for her survival. She was so much better than when she came, so I thought she would manage with a spot of guidance and a lot of faith. She would be at home, stress-free, and fresh air, sunshine, and hard work would help her re-integrate to normal life. I saw the situation from their eyes and was happy to relent.

I promised to talk to Dr. Nisal and arrange for their discharge as soon as possible. She already felt the excitement of going back home. I could see it in her eyes.

48. Shankar

My next patient was in the male ward, the man with the ulcer on the foot. His name was Shankar. And apparently, from the history I gathered he had been visiting our hospital for many months in the past. He had probably met three terms of interns but never carried previous papers as he had lost them. The ulcer was chronic and he had never been tested in detail to understand why the ulcer was not healing.

There was no fever, the breathing was normal, the pulse was good and was well felt in the feet also. The general examination showed the foot ulcer, which was about three inches long and two inches broad at the back of the foot sitting on the Achilles' tendon. The muscles of the feet looked thinned and the skin of the feet had no hair and was dry. Something was amiss. Something was being missed. I couldn't figure out what it could be.

There was something about his face that was peculiar too. His face had less hair and the eyebrows were scanty. Skin was shiny. The hand also had a slightly bony configuration. I stood there thinking. We are dealing with something more than just an ulcer. I have to find the cause.

I asked him to sit on a bench and put his foot on a stool. I squatted on the floor to examine the foot and the ulcer. The foot was unremarkable save the details mentioned earlier. The ulcer was dry, with a fair amount of dead tissue but no active discharge presently.

I cleaned the wound with saline and tried to remove the dead tissue. Some of it came off easily but some I had to cut. Once when I cut the tissue there was bleeding but the patient didn't utter a sound of objection. Stoic? The man is brave, I thought. Normally a patient would be screaming, and whining, and moving the foot away, but Shankar sat through the dressing very peacefully.

I moistened the fresh surface with saline and thereafter put a gauze with soframycin ointment on the wound and closed the wound with a bandage. As a starter I sent his blood for a complete blood count, sugar level and an ESR. More than this we couldn't do in our primitive lab.

I knew that this case was not just an ulcer on the foot. There was much more to it than met the eye.

49. Friends Return

Whilst I was lost in thoughts of Shankar's problem, I missed the commotion near the entrance of the hospital, a few feet away from where I was, squatting on the floor to do the dressing on the foot. Suddenly, there was a sharp thump on my back, pulling me back to reality. I turned, annoyed at this rude interruption...... and the audacity..... "What the he....! Oh! HI GUYS! I never even noticed that you all are back!" Yogendra, Hemant and Hiroo were back. The anger of being rudely interrupted was immediately replaced by the joy of being re-united with friends. Having dressed Shankar's wound I told him that I would come back and talk to him in detail and explain to him the disease and the tests we would have to do. Now that Hiroo and Yogendra, my surgically-oriented friends, were back, we would brain-storm and find an answer to his problem. "How was the journey?"

"It was nice. You know it's nice to get out of the congested and hectic life of Bombay and come to the peace and quiet here."

"Anand, are you homesick now? It's been a month now, hasn't it?"

"More than a month. Hmm.... Not exactly home sick..but yeah.... Been thinking of home and folks quite often these days. Maybe I should go and spend some days at home. Dr. Nisal already gave me the go ahead." It had been a long time and I realised I should go home and look up my family and also get some respite from constant work. The unwitting accident last evening flashed through my mind and again I felt a wave of guilt and regret go over me. I was tired, but my ego prevented me from admitting to any such human weakness. I did need a break, some time away from

151

work, responsibility, stress and irregularity. I need to rest and regroup my inner resources. I noticed the energy and enthusiasm exhibited by my friends which had accrued from a week of staying at home. I decided at that moment that I'd go home for Divali.

"Go after Divali. We'll spend Divali together. After internship we will all go our separate ways. Who knows when we will spend this kind of time together."

"You are right, yaar. Time is just flying and soon we will finish. You guys have already done three months here."

"Really....How time flies. Okay, we are going to the room. You finish the OPD and come soon."

They traipsed off to the room, whilst I settled down to see the few patients waiting for me. Owing to the 'holiday effect' the attendance in the OPD was scant. A rough head count revealed about ten patients. Routine cases featuring coughs, colds, fevers, and a case of gastroenteritis, and vomiting, abdominal pain, and so on.... Two hours had elapsed by the time I sent the last patient away. Just as I was rising to leave the OPD, a man walked in.

50. Near Death

"Sir, we have just arrived by bus, and my friends are bringing the patient in a few minutes." I looked at my watch and noticed that it was already 2 pm. "He has been bitten by a snake and he is very sick," said the stranger.

"What is wrong with him? Is he bleeding ? Or is he weak?"

"Sir, this happened very early in the morning when he had gone into the jungle. He told us about it only after we woke up at 5am. We left home with him immediately to come to the hospital. We were very fortunate to get a bus for the last 30 km or else we would have reached at night. Sir, his legs have become very weak and he is unable to walk."

From this history, it was evident, that he had been bitten by a krait or a cobra whose venom causes neurotoxicity. From the site of the bite the venom gradually spreads along the nerves and paralyses them. First the legs, then the arms, then the facial and neck muscles and finally the muscles responsible for breathing. the intercostal muscles and lastly, the diaphragm. Such patients require ventilatory support for assisted respiration, they need intensive care, they need round-the-clock nursing care, they need.......My mind was racing to assess and respond to the situation. We had none of these facilities. A feeling of severe anxiety seized me. In a reflex, anticipatory move, I came out of the clinic to look outside, wanting to see where the patient had reached.

From the front porch of the hospital we could get a view of the road below and hence, could see anyone approaching the hospital. A few steps away from the main foyer of the hospital and I could get a view of the entire road, right up to the cross-road junction.

There, in the distance, I could see a group of men carrying a man on a bed sheet improvised to be a stretcher. The patient looked motionless. They appeared to be about half a kilometre from the hospital.

I called out to the nurse, urgency in my tone, "Sister, prepare two 20-cc syringes of ASV, one 5% dextrose saline drip, a no.18 scalp vein set, keep the laryngoscope, endotracheal tube and the suction machine ready for use at the bedside. Go sister, get all this ready fast! Ask Maushi to get the endo tube, suction and laryngoscope from the OT."

"Muknya, tu ja. Go and tell the doctors to have lunch soon and come as soon as possible. Tell them a snake bite case with paralysis is getting admitted."

Having mobilised the staff, I was feverishly thinking of the eventualities I will have to prepare for in this case. They were a few steps away from the hospital now. I walked up to meet them. They were all tired and anxious. The patient had a terrified expression on his face. The look of a man faced with imminent death. He was motionless, walking alongside the patient's entourage I asked him to move his legs and show me. He shook his head indicating he couldn't do it. I asked him to raise his arms. He raised them, but the movement was shaky, and ill-sustained. His eyelids were drooping, making him appear sleepy and tired.

Things didn't look good. This patient was in dire straits. We needed to act fast. We transferred the patient to the bed. Sister Shinde and Maushi were attempting to start the IV line. "Sister, start the drip and give him 20cc of ASV stat. Have you got the syringes with 4mgs of decadron and 0.5ml of adrenaline ready?"

"No. I didn't bring those. You never asked me to bring those."

"I might need them in case he breaks out in an allergy. I'm not waiting to give a test dose. Sister have you set the IV line? What happened? Why so long?"

"Can't get the vein. All collapsed." They were digging desperately to find a vein but with no luck.

The patient was so severely dehydrated that his veins had all collapsed. His blood pressure was low. The pulse rate had gone up to 120/minute and the volume was low. "Sister, can't get the vein? Let it be. Give me the ASV. Sister, go and get the adrenaline, and decadron as I said....and HURRY!" I took the syringe and injected the needle under the skin of the abdomen and started pushing the ASV into the subcutaneous space. In the absence of a direct intravenous route this was a good alternative. "Maushi, bring me another syringe with 80cc of ASV urgent!" The first 20 cc went in over two minutes. The patient was rapidly deteriorating. His legs and arms were paralysed. His facial muscles were also paralysed. The abdomen moved up and down in the rhythm of the diaphragm, which was, as yet, free from the effect of the venom. How much more time did I have?

"Sister, bring it soon. Bring me the second injection of ASV! RUN!"

The patient was still maintaining his colour though he was on the brink and could stop breathing any minute. I couldn't wait for that to happen. I had to act FAST! Sister brought me the second lot of ASV...four syringes of 20cc each. I injected the ASV on the abdomen, under the skin. It was a slow route of administration but he didn't have an IV line and I didn't have another choice. The respiratory effort was laboured. I could see the patient using his neck muscles and the diaphragm to breath and I saw frank despair in the patient's eyes.

Hiroo and Yogendra had just arrived. "Yogi, his breathing is going to stop any minute. Grab the endo tube and scope! You are going to have to intubate him. We can then help him to breathe with the ambu bag." I was hoping against hope that we didn't have to face this eventuality. We couldn't possibly ventilate him in this hospital. If things didn't go right then we would have to put the tube and then manually pump air with an ambu bag till he recovered. "Hiroo, the veins are collapsed. Try putting a scalp vein. If you can't, then do a cut-down! I need urgent access for IV fluids. And ASV!"

Hiroo settled down by the bedside, trying to find a vein to lodge the scalp vein needle. A nurse rushed off to the station to bring a venesection tray, in case Hiroo needed to do a cut-down to expose a vein and intubate it with a intravenous catheter to provide an access point for the medications and fluid.

And...Yogendra was readying himself to intubate the patient, if needed.

The patient was drowsy and loosing hold on his consciousness. His speech was slurred and unclear. His breathing was now down to the diaphragm only. One hundred ccs of ASV were already given but there were no signs of any response. Sitting by the bed, one finger on the pulse, I was fixedly staring at the movements of the diaphragm. Up....down.........up...down........up..down. Did I imagine, or were the movements becoming shallower by the moment?

"Hiroo! Yogi! Do you think the breathing is slowing down?"

"Yes. I think he's sinking,'" said Yogendra. Hiroo was intently trying for the venous access.

"Wait! His colour is good and he is rousable. Don't intubate now 'cause he will struggle and gag! Wait till he passes out, then intubate and we will attach the ambu bag." Even as we watched helplessly, the breathing gradually faded to a flicker. He was losing consciousness. In utter dismay, we watched this progression. My heart sinking to my feet. Yogendra looked at me for a signal. He was all set to put the endo tube. Hiroo was still struggling to find a venous access and the patient....was all but lost.

I took a deep breath, raised my hand slowly to signal to Yogendra to put the endo tube as soon as the patient was unconscious. He was on the brink and I lowered my hand signalling the go ahead. Yogi removed the pillow swiftly and extended the patient's neck, inserted the laryngoscope to view the vocal chords so as to enable him to intubate the patient. And every breath in the room was bated in anxiety and suspense!

And....."Wait, wait...wait! Don't put the tube. Look!!" I pointed at the diaphragm incredulously and everyone looked in that direction. A small flicker,...another one. I flashed a glance at the others and I saw them staring, wide-eyed expectation, not even daring to breathe. I quickly focused back to the diaphragm. It was again moving....up......down..up....down...up..down..! There was jubilation! I kept staring hard at the diaphragm as if saying to it. Move!.....move....move, dammit!!

The respiration had certainly restarted. The diaphragm picked up in a few more moments, then the neck, and thereafter, the intercostals. The ASV had worked! In another ten minutes the patient's colour had returned and he was awake.

Everyone in the room was beaming like a 1000 watt bulb. The relief in the room was palpable. More than relief, it was the joy of seeing a near-dead man come back to life. But.....there was still time to rest on our laurels. It could revert and the patient could unexpectedly slip back to the same state of paralysis. Then we would be back to square one and never again so lucky. We still had no IV access and needed to give another 100 cc of ASV over six hours. "Guys, do the cut down. The veins are bad and the scalp vein set is not going to serve us. Need IV access."

The respiration had stabilised and he was breathing better. The fingers had also started twitching, and slight movements at the shoulder and neck muscles were clearly evident. The trunk and lower limbs were also showing signs of coming back to life. The patient was squirming on the bed, desperately trying to move his limbs and trunk. The facial muscles were now moving and the expression on his face was of receding fear and much relief. He could now keep his eyes open too.

"Since he is so conscious now, let's try giving him oral fluids."

"Yes, that's true! We can."

"Okay, let's prop him up and give him a trial with oral fluids." So saying, we grasped him from under his arms and hoisted him to a sitting position. We propped him up with pillows so that he wouldn't slide to either side and fall off the bed. After he was adequately secured we offered him a glass of water which he drank thirstily. There was no gagging or coughing.

"That was nice! No weakness of the swallowing muscles. Sister, give him one more glass of water." The second glass went in easily too. Over the next hour we kept talking to him and giving him water to drink. During this time he not only had a fair amount of water but he told us a lot of his history too.

He was about sixty-five years old and lived with his extended family in a village, 50 km from the hospital. He had a mud hut with a straw thatched roof for a home. They had a small farm, about two acres, on which they grew seasonal produce for their personal consumption and some for sale. Their homestead was very basic and primitive. They went to the well to bathe and to the forest for their ablutions. This morning he went to the forest to relieve himself whilst it was still dark and that's when he was bitten by the snake.

"What is your name, Kaka?"

"Shiva," he said. His lips were parched and tongue was dry. Shiva needed fluids. He was drinking well and, I had no doubts, that if he continued to drink like this, he would be well hydrated in a couple of hours.

In the short span of two hours there was a massive difference in the outlook. Shiva was moving his limbs better and the drooping of his eyelids was imperceptible, but not completely gone. I ordered for another 20 ccs of ASV, pre-empting a deterioration, wrote the notes and orders in the file and then got up to leave. It was nearing 5.30 pm and I suddenly realised....I was starving! I had missed my lunch and now it was time for tea.

51. Some Thoughts and Some Banter

Hemant was sitting on the doorstep with his old, faithful friend, Hema. He had unpacked and brought out a whole lot of goodies sent from home. Vahini had made some tea and...

"Come, Anand, there's a party in the offing!" said Hemant.

I entered to see so many snacks laid out on the table. All of them had brought something from home. I was famished, so I just sat down at the table, grabbed my cup of tea and commenced digging into the snacks. "This food is not going to see the light of another day, guys."

Hot tea and delicious snacks changed the entire mood from sobriety to bonhomie and happiness.

"Drama, yaar! Shiva, gave me a fright. Just as I was going to finish, he landed up. And just as well.......A little more delay and there would have been a another story to tell."

"It's incredible how they reached from so far in the nick of time. So much by bus, so much on foot and, no sooner he reached, he began to collapse."

"It really was dramatic. I was all set to put the tube and you yelled to stop. And the breathing came back so......providentially."

"It's like....he touched death and came back."

"Really."

"Thank God he is well. Had he perished, or had he needed ventilation, we would have been in a royal fix! We would have to sit by his bedside pumping the Ambu bag manually. Can't imagine how we would have managed."

"Hemant, these snacks are great. Please convey my thanks to Aunty."

"Have. You must be very hungry! We have been only eating at home so we are kind of fed up!"

"Ya, home food for seven days. We remembered you often. We knew you must be missing the food."

The chatter went on till six-thirty in the evening and it was soon going to be time for rounds. I realised I had to fill my friends in with the latest ward position. I interrupted the banter saying, "Guys, I have to tell you about three patients I am concerned about."

They all looked at me expectantly and waited for me to speak. I went on to tell them, first, about the patient with the multiple haemangiomata. I described to them his history and my careless, overconfident misjudgement of the diagnosis and resulting blunder in cutting the haemangioma. I told them about the guilt and grief I had felt thereafter. The fact that I had to resort to Dr. Dhande's help and the embarrassment I felt when he saw me in that mess. I told them everything.

Hiroo had been listening intently. He said, "I'll go and see him. From the history I don't think anything further should be done for him. He has so many, they can't be excised. So let's just reassure him. And maybe discharge him. Let me go and see him"

"The second case is a guy with a non-healing ulcer at the back of his foot with no sensation. He has been suffering for the past several months. He needs to immobilise his foot. Yogi, you see him. Tell me what you think should be done."

"The third is Dhavali. She is so much better. The wound is clean and healthy. Still gaping a bit, but better. She wants to go home."

"Hemant. The patients missed their three-eyed doctor. You are the best in the OPD."

"Hahaha. I'll go tomorrow morning and start my OPDs."

The three of them then decided that they would go to the wards and catch up with the work. Since I was free to do what I pleased, I decided to take a long walk.

I changed into my walking attire and set off. This time, not to the lake, but straight on, as far as I felt like going. The light had dimmed into dusk and, far in the distance, the sun was moving over the hills and beyond, only to disappear behind them. The sky was painted in orange hues casting a golden glow over the landscape. A nip in the air heralded the beginning of winter....or the end of autumn. I just walked, following the straight road. Just walked,.... Deep in thought.

I pushed away thoughts of my mistakes. These thoughts kept cropping up every day, at least once a day, and would leave me pensive, regretful, guilty, sad and so negative. I had to shake out of it.

It was nice to have my friends back. They were, or rather, we were a buffer for each other in good times and bad. We had each other for support and for help when we needed. One never felt alone when in each other's company.

Ever since we had come to Jawhar, there had been a sea-change in our attitude to life and matters of every day concern. We lead a simple life like we never did at home. Our present day simplicity could better be termed as frugality. The very basic needs, in clothing, in shelter, in food, and in just about every need of our lives. We had truly imbibed the meaning of living as per our 'needs' and not as per our 'wants'. The distinction between needs and wants is not easily appreciated in a city like Bombay because many wants had insidiously become needs. Most of our frivolous needs had gradually become necessities. Here, in the outbacks, needs are really only needs. Every little thing that we had was an essential item. Essential for survival, essential for health, essential for safety.

As I walked I was marvelling at the amount we all had changed to adapt to the demands of this stint in our careers. We had changed, but never once had a pang of regret. No one ever said he was homesick or that he missed home food or any other aspect of the urban lifestyle. We were truly content and happy here. It was in this state of basic living that we were able to work long hours, to work almost selflessly, and to maintain a modicum of ethical and moral conduct. In this lifestyle of utter simplicity, we were able to front the basic facts of life....of what we needed for survival, of what we needed for existence, of what we needed to be happy. In fact the very concept of happiness became clear to us when we kept our needs to minimum and all our needs were more than satisfied. I was reminded of the thought....a man is as happy as the number of things that he can do without.

Working in such an environment afforded us the realisation that, for subsistence, we need very few things. Simple food, and work to keep busy with, was enough material for a happy life. As the saying goes....Simple living and high thinking. As per this saying we were living exactly the way life was prescribed.

It was in this atmosphere and mindset that, when we received something nice, like Krishna Bhau's sweets, or a cucumber from a grateful patient, or an invitation to the boss' home for dinner or simple hampers of food from home, the joy we experienced was so great. The same things in the city would not afford so much happiness because we already had too much of it without any effort. It's a realisation to know that the fruit of toil is always sweet.

Lost in my quasi-philosophical thoughts, I lost track of time. The walk was therapeutic as always and the solitude in connection with Nature had its own healing influence. By the time I got back it was 8.30 pm.

52. Arm-Chair Ward Rounds

Yogendra, Hiroo and Hemant were waiting for dinner. I washed up and joined them. The walk had again re-ignited my appetite.

"How was your walk."

"Super! I must have walked about 7-8 km. it was refreshing. No one on the road, only an occasional farmer, a chap with his flock of goats, and some villagers returning from work. The road was all mine.

"You don't get bored walking alone."

"No. Never! In fact, I feel best when I am undisturbed and alone. It's the time I set my mind right. Solitude is good for health. Silences the noise inside!" I said pointing a finger at my head and smiling indulgently, waited for my friends to react to my 'high philosophy'.

"Anand, your philosophy is beyond my comprehension. I, frankly, get bored alone. I need company."

"I agree. Can't walk five minutes by myself. Need someone to talk to."

Sitting on the table, in the anteroom, and enjoying a meal together, discussing random subjects just added to the great camaraderie that we shared with each other.

"How was the round? The patients?" I was keen to know how the patients were faring and what they thought on the various cases we had earlier discussed.

Yogendra said, "Shankar will need immobilisation. every time he walks his wound breaks. This is not allowing the wound to heal. I was just thinking...... I will put a plaster on it tomorrow.....but. If I did that the wound will fester inside and that would be self-defeating." Yogendra was thinking aloud and was again lost in thought.

"Yogi, I got an idea. See if it can work. Put the Plaster of Paris cast on his foot. This will immobilise the foot. But before the cast dries up cut a window at the back to expose the wound. Cut from three sides and leave one side hinged to the plaster. You know what I mean? This way, you can keep the foot immobile, and, every once in a while, open the window and look at the wound, put medications, clean or trim the dead tissue, and then again close the window....what do you say?"

"Hey! That's a fantastic idea! A window on the plaster! That's fantastic! I'm going right away to do it." Yogendra was excited with this new, simple innovation.

"I'm coming too," I said, "I'm keen to see how you make this idea work. It just occurred to me."

"Hiroo, what did you talk to the haemangioma patient?"

"His name is Ramya. I talked with him and also saw him in detail. He has multiple haemangiomatosis. Nothing needs to be done. He also agreed and wants to go home tomorrow."

"I'll see tomorrow on my rounds and talk to him."

"He isn't angry or anything? After all the explanation he was very accepting and he, himself, suggested that he be allowed to go home. I will fill the discharge card tomorrow."

"Okay. How is Shiva."

"He is very well. His limbs are all moving normally, his breathing, swallowing and speech are all normal. He just has some residual weakness. He is well hydrated and had a full dinner too. We haven't had to give anymore ASV. Maybe, if all is well, tomorrow we can send him home."

"Wow! It feels good to know that he is better from what he was when he came here. Snake bite cases can be dramatic in every way conceivable."

"Dhavali wants to go home but I feel she should stay till she is completely okay. But then, it's their wish to go home, so I think we should let them go tomorrow."

"Okay. So it is three discharges tomorrow."

"Yogi. Do you really want to do the plaster tonight?"

He thought awhile and then said, "Okay, tomorrow!"

I guess we were all tired. It had been an eventful and gratifying day.

53. Heart to Heart

It had been a long postponed thought in my mind that I must talk to Dhavali and her husband and find out how she got into this mess. Today was a light day as we were four and there wasn't so much to do as yet. And there was my eternal nemesis of the past few days.... Ramya... I had to talk to him too. I had to talk to Ramya more to assuage my feelings than to give him any reassurance. Hiroo had done a great job of that already.

With this resolve I left with the others for the ward. Hemant and Hiroo for the OPD. Yogendra for the plaster he was so keen to do.....and I left for the two important one-on-one meetings I had planned on doing.

I headed straight for Ramya's bed. As I approached the ward i saw Ramya sitting on the bed, looking pensive. He was obviously in deep thought. The dressing on his ear stood out prominently, a sordid and painful reminder of my folly. I stood by the bed and waited for him to look up before I spoke to him. He looked up almost immediately and smiled broadly. He was happy to see me after a lapse of two days. He must have been waiting for me to come and tell him what happened and what he should do next.

There was not a hint of rancour, or remorse, or regret, that something wrong had been done to him. In fact, he may not have been aware that something wrong may have been done.

"Ramya," I said, "I'm sorry I was unable to come to see you for two days. I was busy with a problem."

"No problem, Sir. I can understand. The other doctor had come yesterday and the nurses have been looking after me so well."

This was the beauty of the Adivasi temperament. They were so immensely forgiving. They had so much tolerance, forbearance, faith, loyalty and devotion towards those whom they loved. In my experience, whether it was Ramya, or Dhavali, or Potya, or Shankar, or Laxmi...it didn't matter, they were all the same. They went through tough times and recovered or were still unwell to a certain extent and were on the track to full recovery, whatever the case was, they were a hundred percent with us and for us. Their gratitude was paramount and unparalleled. In suffering, they had grit, tenacity and resilience and in gratitude, they gave from their heart.

The look on Ramya's face spoke the same emotions. There was not a trace of misgiving. Putting a hand on his shoulder, I looked him straight in the eyes and explained to him everything about his problem. I told him about the misjudged nature of the swelling and how I had operated on him thinking it was something else.

What had turned out was actually something totally different. I further told him that the lumps were too widespread to be able to remove them all...and that removing them all was not necessary as they were simple, harmless swellings. I also told him that this was a very rare problem and that very few had it. He listened with wide- eyed awe and rapt attention. He was taking in every word I said. I had spoken to him in the very basic vernacular language so that he could understand the problem clearly and to learn to live with the problem. At the end of half an hour, I had satisfied every query he had. He asked me if he could stay till the stitches were removed. I thought that was a good idea and consented without a second thought. With a sense of fulfilment and satisfaction I left his bedside.

As I was heading for Dhavali's bed I ran into Yogendra who called out excitedly. He was with Shankar, working on his foot plaster. He was keen to share his handiwork. He had devised an ingenious dressing for Shankar's foot. He placed a POP cast on the entire foot to immobilise the ankle joint. This would eliminate all movement and allow the ulcer at the back of the foot to heal undisturbed. Further, in order to gain access to the wound, at the back of the foot, over the Achilles' tendon, he had cut out a window in the plaster before it had dried up and set into hardness. This was like a flap and could open back and forth like a window.

"This is super, Yogi! Professional job!"

"It is going to be my profession so it better be the best," he said, with pride in his voice. The execution of our idea last night was perfect and would now help the patient to heal without much delay. Moreover, with this plaster it would now not be necessary to immobilise the patient, and he would be free to move about as he pleased.

I left Yogendra to put his finishing touches as I moved on to Dhavali's bed. She was cutting gauze pieces and packing them into brown envelopes. This was the least intensive and most needed activity in the ward. Her help was going a long way in keeping up our ever-dwindling stocks of gauze. So many patients in the ward and the OPD needed dressings every day and, for them, all the stocks were being used up even as they were being replenished. Her help took the burden off the nurses' shoulders and now, they could use their time more profitably for the patients. Keeping Dhavali gainfully occupied was serving well to help her forget her recent tragedy and get back into mainstream life. Grief is a silent killer that saps mental energy that is so vital in helping the body to heal from any insult, whether it be mental or physical. From a distance, I watched Dhavali working on her bed, engrossed in her activity. I could see clearly, how much she had improved from the time when she was brought to us. Her haemoglobin was almost in double figures, the swelling had gone, the infection had been overcome, her appetite was good, she slept well, and her mental make up was more at peace with herself and the environment.

I approached her bedside quietly, not wanting to disturb her concentration and complete involvement in her work. I stood there for a minute before she realised I was by her side. As soon she saw me, she stopped her work and looked up.

"Namaskar, Dhavali. Kashi hai? How are you?" I greeted her. She returned my greeting with her smile. That was when I was struck by the pure whiteness of her teeth. I couldn't help marvel at the fact that, though her teeth were crookedly aligned, they were like shining pearls. She may have been described as unattractive, but when she smiled she actually lit up and looked good. Her smile was radiant. That was her best ornament.

For the next half an hour Dhavali and I talked about her life, her health, her likes, her dislikes, and other issues, in an attempt to understand how and why she had landed in this dire predicament. She was loathe to open up at first, but once the flood gates opened, there was a torrent that kept flowing unprovoked. She let out everything that she had held inside her. She spoke to me for the next half an hour, uninterrupted, her tone even, her eyes honest and steady, and her demeanour poised and graceful.

Her story was a story from the pages of a tragic novel set in the midst of economic poverty, but a profound wealth of spirit and determination.

54. Dhavali's Story

Dhavali and her husband Satya, were married four years ago. Soon after they married, Satya's parents passed away in a span of one year. Both of them had suffered infections following injuries sustained whilst working. From the descriptions of the symptoms, his father had probably died of tetanus, and his mother from a fulminating infection on her foot which had spread upwards and had involved her entire lower limb. Both had died due to the absence of good medical care nearby.

Satya, who was a farmer, with a small plot of land which he cultivated for a livelihood, had not realised that he should take his parents to the big hospitals as soon as they were ill. His father was a healthy man who worked hard. One day, whilst working in the field, he sustained an injury on his foot with a hoe and within a day it had festered, and after four days he had stiffness of the body, Satya never once suspected that this stiffness was ominous and that he should have taken expert medical advice and treatment.

His father was at home when the stiffness rapidly progressed to cause him a locked jaw and difficulty in breathing. It was then that Satya realised that something was seriously wrong. But alas!....It was too late. By the time he mustered the means to take his father to the hospital about sixty kilometres away, he had gone into a severe state of stiffness and soon breathed his last. For Satya and his family, that was a devastating blow. A working man, a bread- winner, is suddenly no more. An Adivasi family that loses a bread- winner, goes through the most serious upheavals one can ever imagine. Satya went through the throes of bereavement over the next few months whence he tried to find his bearings and take over the reins of his family.

Life was tough for him and his family. He had to find work wherever it was available and many a times he had to stay away from home for a few days. During these periods, Dhavali looked after their small farm and Satya's mother looked after the household. Satya had to stay away from home far too often in search of work and Dhavali had to work hard on their farm. On one fateful day, Satya's mother, whilst cooking, spilt some hot oil on her foot when she lost her balance and tipped the oil containing utensil off the stove. The hot oil scalded her foot causing deep burns on the upper surface. Dhavali had poured cold water on the affected part in an attempt to mitigate the damage, but the damage was done. The wound festered and the infection spread upwards. Satya was away from home at that time. When he returned his mother was critically sick and Dhavali was also on the brink of exhaustion. Satya's mother died after a few days.

The two deaths left the young couple shattered and they went into hibernation and grieved for several months. It was about that time when Dhavali conceived her twins. She was weak to start with, but as the pregnancy progressed, she became weaker and weaker. She was pale and started manifesting swelling on her feet. In the seventh month of her pregnancy she was not eating at all, had swelling all over her body, and was so weak that she could hardly rise from the floor. Satya tried hard to feed her with whatever he could get from other farms. She needed a doctor he realised, and was planning to take her soon. The hospital, however, was far.

Soon she was into her eighth month and completely bed-ridden. She looked extremely large. However, when she went into labour all of a sudden, and things took a turn for the worst, he had no time to arrange for any proper transport to take her to the hospital. On that ill-fated night, he mustered all his courage, and decided to just start moving, hoping against hope for some help along the way. He walked with her and when she was tired, he carried her on his back but the large abdomen and the swelling made it very difficult for him to carry her. It was slow and laborious, and with the relentless downpour life couldn't have been more trying for Satya, and Dhavali.

In this state, they had reached the cottage hospital in the late evening, where we had taken charge of her treatment. It must have been Divine Grace that reached them to the hospital on that night after such an arduous journey,

After having told me the full story, she looked down at the floor. She was crying silent tears. She had opened up her heart and she had exposed her wounds. I realised now, what they had gone through in their short life together. Maybe it was the time to bounce back now. Maybe this was the turning point in their cycle. It was the time to rebuild the broken pieces of a tough, unrelenting, uncompromising life. They had seen the worst and now things could only get better. Dhavali was crying. The flood, suppressed thus far, was flowing freely. There was no point in stopping it now. Henceforth, she was going to resurrect both their lives. She would now script the better chapters in their life together.

We bought a month's supply of vitamins and protein supplements and prepared to discharge her the next day. She promised me that she would return in a month, completely healed. She was going to take care of herself, she was going to be brave and she was going to face adversity with equanimity.

55. An Emotional Farewell

The next day was a busy day. After breakfast we all headed for the maternity ward. Dhavali and Satya were about to leave for their home. Dhavali was beaming in anticipation. There was a sea change in her health and her general outlook. There was such a huge difference between what she was when she first came here and what she was today at the time of her going home. She was probably in the best health she ever was in the past four or more years.

She bid farewell to every staff member and doctor personally. The staff, on their part, had all gathered near the entrance to see her off. There were some emotional moments, especially between the staff and her. She was more than just a case to many of us. She had, in her stay at the hospital, stretched the limit of the medical ethic, and the medical norms. Everything about her had crossed the conventional boundaries.

Dhavali and Satya finally left and the staff returned to their work. A sense of emptiness prevailed in every heart. She had, most certainly found a place in the hearts of all who worked at the hospital.

The rest of the day was routine.

56. Going Home

The next week passed in a blur of routine activity. The OPDs were heavy as the holidays were over. The admissions were routine cases, many snake bite cases but none with manifest complications. They would receive their dose of ASV and would be discharged the next day. Snake bites were more common in and after the monsoons as the grass grew tall and the snakes hid in the grass. Generally someone would accidentally step on or disturb a lurking snake and it would lash out in self defence. in most cases, if not all, the history was similar.

There were many deliveries as always. All were normal and uncomplicated. Surgeries were restricted to the vasectomies that Dr. Dhande performed. Occasionally a wound had to be attended to by one of us.

We had many walks, both on the trail that lead to the dam and on the road to the Hanuman Temple and the Sunset Point. On days when we wanted to break the monotony of repetitive work, we would go to the market and buy supplies and then walk on the road to the Hanuman Temple and after visiting the Temple we would have a brief interlude with the sunset at Sunset Point. The Sunset Point afforded us an outstanding view of the valley below and the setting sun, playing with the colours in the sky and finally sinking into the distant mountains to disappear leaving the soft afterglow of twilight followed very soon by the silvery hues of night. Then we would walk back in the semi darkness and regale at the sight of hundreds of glow worms crawling on the roads.

There was no other entertainment in Jawhar save what we created amongst ourselves. One of our favourite entertainments was to build a bonfire and sit around it and tell stories. These sessions invariably turned into laugh riots. Yogendra had some working knowledge of astronomy and on clear nights he would entertain us with his knowledge of stars and constellations. The Hunter, The Arrow and the The Lion were what I remember till date. The Hunter was a very bright star. Juxtaposed with the Hunter, there was a line of stars which resembled an Arrow shot by the Hunter, and the Lion was an asymmetrical quadrilateral of stars. The rest of the astronomy class went over my head as I couldn't see what they saw.

Divali was approaching and the town wore a festive look. Shops had put up colourful lights which brightened the otherwise drab evening skyline. Even the staff of our hospital had decorated the front entrance with lamps and lights of different colours enlivening the atmosphere significantly. There were no plans for Divali and I had some leave sanctioned by Dr. Nisal. Maybe I should go home.

I made my way to Dr. Nisal's office.

"Sir?"

"Yes, Anand?"

Sir, you recall saying that I should go home for a break? Well, I have been thinking about it and realise I want to do that. Would you mind if I went home for a week? Hiroo, Yogendra and Hemant are here and Dadan and Syed may also come."

"Go, Anand, you must be needing it."

"Thank you so much, Sir. I'll go the day after Divali."

"Why after Divali? Go and spend Divali with your family."

"Leave tomorrow and return by the end of the month."

"That's 13 days, Sir," I said, doing some quick maths in my head. "That's too long."

"It's okay, Anand. You have worked very hard in the last one month. You must take a break lest your judgement gets impaired.

If you don't take breaks you will lose interest in your work and your health will start deteriorating.

"Okay, Sir. I will leave tomorrow."

I shared the news with the friends and they said, "Why wait till tomorrow? If there is a bus today, go!"

It was 12 noon. There was a bus at 3 pm. Great! I packed my bag quickly and after lunch I left for the bus stop. Strangely, there was a kind of happiness stemming from the thought of being homeward bound once again.

57. Bombay

I boarded the bus and settled down in my seat. Partially oblivious of the chatter around me. I could hear it like static disturbance on a radio but my mind was on the days ahead. The bus journey was uneventful and we reached Bombay Central bus depot when it was already dark.

In sharp contrast to the tranquility in Jawhar, the city was bustling with activity. The roads were chock-a-block with vehicles always in a hurry to reach somewhere, honking incessantly, assaulting the eardrums mercilessly. Handcarts selling wares, people walking, roadside shops and squatters added to the pulsating atmosphere of the heart of Bombay city. I don't know whether I was glad to arrive to this city I called home or was there an unspoken aversion already brewing in my heart.

I picked up my bag and alighted from the bus, my eyes searching for a taxi. Found it. A ten minute drive later, I was home. Coming home had a 'butterflies in the stomach' feeling. It was after a month and more that I was returning, and I hadn't had any contact in the intervening period. My parents were surprised and overjoyed when I entered. Ten thousand questions. How was your work? How was the climate? Were there mosquitoes? Did you eat? Did you sleep? Did you have too much work? How long is the travel? You look so tired.... Have you had dinner?.........and it continued unabated. Parental concern. Whilst being shot down by question gun-fire, I walked into my bedroom. It seemed strange to walk back into the lap of luxury after being in the wilderness. I looked around my room. Nothing had changed but my perspective had changed. When I had returned from England my room had looked simple yet inviting.

My reaction to returning to Bombay, after being in England for six weeks, had been a tad averse, given the fact that Bombay was a noisy, dirty, disorganised city where the infrastructure had always been stretched to the limits and veritably bursting at the seams. The midnight arrival at the airport was depressing at best, especially when one steps out into the city. On the flip side, returning to Bombay from Jawhar had the same dirty feeling, but coming home had a dream-like feeling. Of being in my room, my bed, my toilet, my home. The contrast could be good or bad depending on which perspective one held and what it was relative to. Everything in life is relative. Light-dark, day-night, black-white, good-bad everything had a different meaning relative to what you compared it with. This realisation hit me as soon as I entered my room.

My mother rushed off to the kitchen to see what she could conjure up for dinner. I put down my bag and stepped into the bathroom. What a difference from what we had in Jawhar!...and how we had gotten used to the state of affairs in Jawhar? It is indeed incredible how the human mind gets used to anything, hardship or comfort and how easily he makes the adaptation to survive.

"Mummy, don't bother. I'll make myself an omelette. We have bread I hope?"

"Sorry, Anand, since you both (my brother and i) are not at home, I have not stocked any bread. I have some chapatis and thepla, if you want."

"Okay, whatever is there. Don't worry."

I made the omelette and whilst eating dinner I sat with my parents and filled them in on my latest adventures in Jawhar. They were amazed to hear the stories of the kind of work we were doing, and it was in the wee hours of the morning that we decided to sleep.

The week was a complete antithesis of life in Jawhar.

I visited my alma mater, JJ. Hospital, and found my friends in the Central Canteen. The Central Canteen was the 'hangout' zone for anyone who had nothing to do and wished to eat, meet friends or just pass some time listening to chatter and music. The CC as it was called had a vibrant ambience and was a lively place, made even livelier by a juke box, where we could play the songs of our choice for a small consideration. Sometimes the same song played again and again when the same popular song was requested by every new entrant to the CC. It was lunch time and I was lucky to find my friends sitting on a large table. There was a round of greetings and excitement as I pulled up a chair to join them. The next few hours were filled with animated conversations of what was happening in our lives.

It was nearing 3 pm and our group had dwindled to four of us. "What's the plan now?"

"Nothing really."

"Let's go for a movie? Umrao Jaan, Ek duuje ke liye? Which one?"

Looking at my watch I said,"What time is the show?"

"At 4 pm. Shall we go?

"Ok let's go." All of us rose. We took a taxi to the centre of town where Umrao Jaan was playing. The movie was different from the normal commercial films. The music and acting were both outstanding. It was nice sitting in a cinema hall and watching a nice movie after so long. The charm of having popcorn in the intermission, discussing the movie after it was over, glossing over how beautiful the protagonist lady was! And how every moment added to the net worth of the price of the ticket which was Rs. 3.50/-

"Good choice. Nice movie."

"Wow. The days gone by. Got to get home now."

I got home in time for dinner and over dinner had more talk with the family. Stories of Jawhar and the questions arising from the stories were countless. However, all the comments were not good. Some were critical and evoked many admonitions in true parental fashion. Some of the stories met with approval and pride. The parents were quite amazed how their city-bred son has managed so well in a remote village with no prior experience nor priming. Some things were just ordained to be as they were.

The next few days were spent in catching up with school friends and meeting relatives. Days were fun, meeting friends and listening to their stories was exciting, but when they heard of what we were doing, they too were amazed. In sharp contrast to the fun-filled and frivolous lives that they lived in the city, under the garb of relaxation or 'chilling', we were actually trying to make a difference in people's lives and health and, in the bargain, making a huge difference in our own lives. In one month, I felt that I may have matured by ten years. Life in Bombay was colourful, vivacious, extraordinary. It was pulsating with frenetic activity but, the activity, sadly, lacked direction or purpose.

Divali, was an extravaganza of sweet, colourful lights, new clothes, socialising, food, and presents,....But above all else was Sound!......Noise!......Explosive, deafening senseless noise! And smoke and pollution......and even above that. HEAT! October heat in Bombay is legendary! Even hotter and more sultry than summer. And to wear the fineries in this heat and then compound it with needless firecrackers which added to the heat was, to my mind an exercise in futility. I often wondered in my life...WHY did Divali come in the worst season in Bombay. It would have been so much more fun to enjoy good food and entertain with friends if the climate was good. What was the need for this cruelty, perpetrated under the garb of religion?

The days of Divali and New Year were packed with socialising and seemed never to end. Tired of eating, talking, smiling, sweating, and travelling from house to house, I finally came to the end of my leave. I can't say it was all a bad experience. There were plenty of moments of fun too. The same activity in a cold climate would have been truly superb. But....Nevertheless, we had a good time and now it was time to go.

Refreshed and rejuvenated, and fully stocked-up, I left for Jawhar on the 30th of October by the 6.15 am bus.

58. Back in Jawhar

Getting back was so good. The old enthusiasm, the old energy, the old killer-instinct were all back. This arrival was not fraught with stress as were the previous two arrivals. This one was almost akin to a kind of home-coming. The climate in Jawhar was getting cooler and though it was nearing noon, there was a cool breeze along the way to the hospital. On reaching the hospital I made for the OPD, where I was sure Hemant and Hiroo must be. They were there, surrounded by a few patients.

"Hi, guys," I said. They smiled back and waved, signalling that they were almost done with the OPD, and that they would meet me in the room. On the way, I saw Yogendra and Dadan at work in the wards. It was nice to be back. The sisters on duty also waved and wished me a Happy Divali. I returned their greeting with a smile.

Back in the room, I placed my bag and dropped onto the bed. The peace and quiet in the room and the fatigue of the journey suddenly got the better of me. As I lay down and shut my eyes I must have drifted off to sleep because the next thing I knew was Dadan shaking me gently and calling out. I surfaced to realise that it was 1.30 and time for lunch. Whilst having lunch we caught up on the news. I told them of my week in Bombay and they filled me in on what had transpired in Jawhar. Essentially the work was routine. Nothing out of the ordinary. We decided that, this evening, we would build a bonfire and have dinner out in the open. After lunch, Dadan and I slipped off to the region behind the hospital to look for firewood. It felt exactly like times of yore when the hunter-gatherer would go out into the wilderness to gather firewood and then, on the fire, he would cook his meal. We gathered quite a bit of wood and were excited about having a long bonfire session.

Vahini planned to cook us a nice dinner. She gave us the menu and it sounded great. We also asked her for ten to twelve potatoes which we planned to roast in the fire. Unfortunately we had no skewers to make a kind of barbecue but this was more than enough. The day wore on. At six we all decided to settle down and build the fire. Hemant brought the chairs out and arranged them in a circle around the designated spot. Hiroo and I arranged the logs of wood and having done that, ignited the thin, dry twigs in the centre which quickly caught fire. As the twigs ignited the bigger sticks caught fire and then the logs. The crackling fire exuded a welcome warmth as the climate began to chill after sunset. It was a lively evening and soon all was set.

"Hey, did you know that there is going to be an eye camp on the next weekend at the school," and he pointed at the municipal secondary school across the meadow. The school was an old British colonial style building on the same lines as the external facade of the cottage hospital. They had a huge playground on which would be parked the mobile vans for surgery. And the patients will be housed in the open on hired mattresses and shelters. It was a big project sponsored and initiated by the Rotary club.

"How will they conduct it. Any idea?'"

"They have sent a car with a loudspeaker across all the villages in the vicinity blaring news of the camp and inviting villagers who have diminished vision to come and get themselves assessed."

"Does that work? Do people come? Is it free?"

"It must be free with Rotary sponsoring the camp. Surgeons come and oblige the club and give their services pro bono."

"Three surgeons will operate on all of them. Three vans will be used simultaneously on that day. The aim is to do at least 100 patients in a day."

"Wow! Is that possible. About 33 patients per surgeon. In let's say 8 hours? Or ten hours? and....They can't work non-stop. They will take breaks......So about one and half hours in breaks? That leaves eight and a half hours. Then take out another hour for food and toilet. So seven and a half hours that is .... 450 minutes ...and divide that by 33 equals. .... Ummmm.... That comes to 13 and a half minute per patient. Bull-shit! How the hell can you do such a delicate surgery in that much time."

After that insightful outburst every one was quiet and deep in thought. Suddenly the atmosphere had become serious.

"Hey guys! You've become serious yaar!"

"It's a serious matter, yaar. How can they do this to the poor people. Just to show that they did social work. they come here and call the press, people click photos and do these many surgeries. Does anybody follow the patient and see what the long term outcome is? They should do that."

"These camps are all useless and only publicity stunts to show that they did social service."

"Bloody bull.....! They want bulk.... We did hundred.!!... How many got screwed up? No one knows. Let someone come and see how many got ruined, infected, lost their vision."

"Why don't you do that research?" was the gentle suggestion to the young and enthusiastic renegade. "The day after the surgery you go and see all the patients and see if they had their medications, put their drops, keep the eye clean and finally check them ten days later to see if they had healed well and whether at the end of a month they get special glasses."

"But there was no assuaging his indignant feelings. He was on fire. "All camps are eye wash and a hoax. Bloody bullshit!"

"No, yaar. All camps are not like that. Some really do good for the community. This camp too may do good for the community.

Why don't you really do that research, and if not, then why not just wait and watch? And see what happens."

As this discussion was heating up, Vahini arrived and announced, "Dinner is ready."

That's when we all realised we were really hungry. The dry climate of the hills did wonders for our appetites. We all trouped into the house to fill our plates. The food was well made and fragrant. We loaded our plates and returned to the bonfire which was still glowing steadily. The potatoes in the fire were well charred. We fished them out and, after peeling them we buttered the cut ends. There were enough for all of us. Delicious.

Sitting around the fire, we finished dinner, talked a lot and finally as the embers were dying and the glow fading, sleep crept in surreptitiously. Before sleep supervened, we made one more dig at our colleague....

"We have lots to do. From tomorrow we have to write a paper on the post-op complications of cataract surgery in non-domiciliary conditions. We have to crack the conspiracy of the rich against the poor!"

"Shut up!" He turned his back to us in indignation and slept. We followed suit ...amused with his self-righteous anger.

59. The Eye Camp

The weekend arrived and the mobile vans rolled in. There were close to two hundred people gathered there for the eye camp. Of these about sixty patients would be short- listed for surgery. The rest were the support system in the form of family and friends.

True to their culture, no Adivasi went for a surgery by himself. He always had at least two, if not more, people accompanying him for help and security. They really cared for each other and therefore, there was never a dearth of people ready to offer their time and efforts.

We could see the activity at the camp from our quarters. We had never seen so many people around the school in the past two months. It was a milling crowd. Tarpaulin tents had been erected to house the patients. There were not enough tents for all the patients. Hence many of them were accommodated on thin mattresses lined up in the open. The climate being pleasant, it wasn't uncomfortable. They were used to sleeping in the open in good weather, and when they stayed up in the nights to watch over their crops. So this may not have been a new experience for them, but it was, most certainly, a new experience for us, to see them being housed in the open. Our young and militant minds took offence at such gross neglect. We were forming an opinion in our minds, albeit a prejudicial opinion. As on-lookers from a distance, we were assuming that these poor patients were being treated callously and summarily.

In the crowd there were the Rotarians who looked distinctly different in their city attire, there were the patients who were sitting, with their eyes closed, ostensibly to dilate the pupils before full ophthalmic evaluation and surgery, and there were the relatives who were scurrying around trying to be of help to one another. The activity carried on through the morning, till late in the afternoon. The surgeries were all done by six in the evening after which the surgeons and the Rotarians left the venue. I asked Dadan if he wanted to come across with me to meet the patients and see how they were faring. He was instantly agreeable to the idea and was up saying,"Come. Let's go!"

"Take your torch along."

"Yes. Taken."

We walked across the distance to the school. Dusk had set in and the twilight made the visibility poor. We approached the first patient and asked, "How are you?"

"Theek aahe. I'm fine. A little....pricking pain."

"Okay."

The next patient, "How are you?"

"I am fine. Though I have a pricking sensation like a mild pain in my eye. And there is a feeling of constant wetness."

"Did anyone come and see you? Did you get any medications or eye drops?"

"They haven't given me any medications. They just put some ointment in my eye at the time of surgery and said that now they will see me tomorrow."

"See, this is how they neglect the patients. No drops, no post-op care!"

"Really! How careless on their part."

We must have seen about thirty patients in this manner and drew our own conclusions as to how these folk should have been managed. The next day saw the doctors return to examine the patients. The patients were given the protective pads, and the spectacles and a bottle of drops and, after giving them instructions on how to use them, they were sent home. We continued to nurture the feeling, self derived and self created, that the Rotary club and the doctors had been very callous and had neglected the patients. We discussed our feelings over many a cup of tea, and were getting firmer of opinion, day by day, that the entire camp was a hoax.

Till.......three weeks later,......

The patients operated at the camp started coming back to us for a follow up. I saw more than ten of them and all had healed well with a large proportion reporting significant improvement in their vision. They had no post-op congestion or swelling. No complaints. It was, indeed, remarkable to see them return so satisfied and happy. The patients had changed my opinion of the camp and I realised that, in these camps, the surgeons tried their best to give the patients relief, and that we, as spectators, should have offered help rather than having criticised them and formed negative opinions regarding the entire activity. We were prejudiced and cynical. It was our weakness and folly.

The overall outcome of this camp was excellent. So many had gained good vision and had improved prospects for a better quality of life. We were wrong in criticising them.

"The camp patients came today for follow-up. They seem to be doing well."

"Ya, I saw some too. They had no complications. Can't even tell that they had a surgery......and we were criticising them wholesale! Really......."

"It's our inherent trait. If we are not part of a good venture we find something wrong with it and magnify the wrong in our minds. The truth is....We can't stand someone's success unless it includes us.

So when we are not a part of it, we are against it. And so we tear it to shreds with nary a second thought. We must be a very prejudiced culture!"

"True. Well said."

Our thought processes, our prejudices, our inherent jealousies. our unwarranted, pseudo self-righteousness was suddenly on the anvil of scrutiny. An objective look at what we had thought and said two weeks earlier, suddenly seemed to shame us. It was not a trait peculiar to just us. it was a trait of the community we lived in. It probably stemmed from a deep-seated jealousy of another's success and happiness,

Prejudice was a poison that we were unwittingly nurturing in our daily transactions, whether with our loved ones, or with our contemporaries at work, or in the society at large. It was this very prejudice that prompted us to look for flaws in an otherwise altruistic project to help the needy find good vision. This realisation dawned on us at a time when we were still open to change. As raw interns, we still had the temerity to change, if found wanting.

Prejudice was there as an in-built habit, but pride had not gripped us yet, we discussed our folly till late that night. It was a night of philosophical rumination and imminent change. for the better.

60. Twelve Hours Apart!

Hiroo and Hemant were going to return to Mumbai. Yogendra, Dadan and I would remain at the hospital. The climate was salubrious, the illnesses less and hence the patient load was manageable. The clinic saw a steady stream of patients unlike the overload of monsoon and summer.

On one such day, Dadan and Yogendra were in the OPD and I was taking ward rounds, when Mukne rushed into the ward and exclaimed, "Sir! Sir! Quick! There is a patient at the entrance in a bullock cart! She looks very sick."

I hurried to the entrance. There was a bullock cart parked outside the entrance around which a crowd had gathered. They seemed to be trying to get a patient out of the cart very carefully, On going up to the cart I saw a scene that I will never, in my lifetime, ever forget. There, on the floor of the cart, was this young woman, lying exhausted, with blood between her legs and the cotton sheet on which she lay.....and....reposed in that blood, oblivious of the gravity of the situation, was this cherubic, healthy baby, still connected to the umbilical cord! The baby boy was happily thrashing his limbs and gurgling peacefully. The mother's abdomen was still distended. The sight was heart wrenching!.

I summoned Mukne, and others assembled around the cart, to quickly carry the patient to the labour ward on the same bed sheet on which she had been brought here to the hospital. I called out to Maushi whilst rushing to the labour ward behind the entourage. A quick look at her abdomen revealed that there was another baby inside. The thrashing of the limbs could be felt on touching the abdomen.

"Twins!" There was an astonished look on everyone's face. There was excitement rife in the labour ward.

Maushi asked the patient, "When did the first one come out?"

"Last night, At about 9 pm,." she gasped, her voice hoarse from exhaustion." "But...after that.....the midwife.......was confused..... because.......the abdomen.......uh...was still....distended. She said there was.......another baby......inside,....and that she didn't....know ....how..... And what should be done....to get that one out...uh ..uh. So...... my family decided......to bring..... me....to this hospital."

"Okay. Got it."

Her pulse rate was 110/minute, respiration rate was 40/ minute, her blood pressure was 80/50 mmHg. She was pale and exhausted to the point of collapse. The abdomen was distended and tense and the baby was lying horizontally. We had no other choice, "Maushi! Cut the cord! It has been connected for more than twelve hours." Maushi ligated the umbilical cord at two points adjacent to each other, with suture material, and cut the cord between the two ligatures. The baby, hitherto attached to the mother, was now free and independent. Without an iota of doubt the boy was a perfect ten on the APGAR score. The infant was whisked away by Sister Shinde to be cleaned and wrapped in white cotton towels.

"Sister, please call Dadan and Yogendra."

"Calling."

"What shall we do next?" I asked this question more to myself than to anyone in particular. Maushi interjected, "Let's do internal version. She has a transverse lie and delivery will be difficult in that position. Her labour has already been so prolonged. We must do something soon. Shall I? Internal version?"

"Maushi, you mean put your hand into the uterus and turn the baby? Have you ever done that before?"

"Yes. Several times."

"How is it done? I haven't seen it being done."

"Just see......" so saying, she donned a pair of sterile gloves and put her hand gently into the vagina. Her hands were small. She herself was a diminutive, 4'8" lady and her hands were like those of a seven or eight year old girl. She gently inched her way upwards into the birth canal and with her other hand on the outside of the abdomen she guided the head of the baby towards the lower end of the uterus. With some gentle coaxing, the baby gradually turned and the head started coming down into the birth canal.

"Maushi, fantastic! You are the best!"

Slowly, painstakingly, she manipulated the baby's head to the birth canal and as soon as she was sure the head was down, she said, "Doctor, order the Pitocin drip."

"Start the drip, Sister," I said to Sister Shinde who had returned to the patient after cleaning and wrapping the baby. She broke an ampoule of Pitocin and added it to a bottle of 5% dextrose. She started the drip and, in a few minutes, the uterus started contracting. The contracting uterus pushed the baby down, thus engaging the head in the birth canal, thereby locking the baby in that position. Maushi removed her hand gently from the vagina, a look of satisfaction on her countenance. The baby would be born in a few moments from now.

As the pains mounted the exhausted mother made a big effort to push the baby out. She summoned all her reserves of energy and, in synchrony with the encouraging calls of the labour ward staff, she gave one final heave and the baby descended. The crown with its patch of black hair was soon visible at the mouth of the birth canal. Sister Shinde called out excitedly," The baby is crowning!........PUSH, come on! LAST TIME....PUSH,".... And with one last heave, and with Maushi's expert fingers helping, the baby's head popped out. Maushi gently eased the head out and putting a finger in the baby's armpit she hooked the shoulder and pulled it out followed by the arm and then she gently pulled the baby out.

Almost instantly the baby cried,... and cried lustily. One look at the baby and Maushi exclaimed, "Another boy!" The mother was beaming despite her pain and tiredness. The second brat was also a perfect ten on the APGAR score. About thirty minutes later the placenta was delivered. There was one placenta with two umbilical cords. The midwife in the village was a wise old lady, she could have killed the second baby had she tried to force the placental delivery after the first baby. She knew where her limits were and when she must refer the case to a hospital.

There was jubilation in the atmosphere of the labour ward with the husband now having joined us. Both parents of the identical twins were overjoyed and couldn't conceal it. There were celebrations outside where the relatives burst into spontaneous applause when they were informed by the father.

"What is your name, Tai?" In my hurry to get the delivery done and ease her from her imminent problems, I had forgotten to ask for her name and so also to inform Dr. Nisal of this difficult delivery.

"Paru." The exhausted mother replied in a weak whisper.

"Sleep Parubai, everything is fine."

No sooner the babies had been settled and the mother had been administered a dose of Methergin to stop excessive bleeding in the post delivery period, I left the labour ward to inform Dr. Nisal.

Yogendra and Dadan were approaching the labour ward, so I called out to them to tell them the good news. "Arre yaar, twins! And that too, twelve hours apart."

"Wow! Same, same?" Dadan said with a twinkle in his eye, referring to the identical twins.

"Ya, same, same!" I replied, smiling broadly. "Can you please go and watch over them. I'm going to tell Dr. Nisal."

"Sure,"said Yogendra.

I walked over to Dr. Nisal's office and, after knocking on the door, entered. He looked up as I entered. "Yes, Anand?"

"Sir, we just received a patient who came from Wada. A female about 27-years old, pregnant, at term, she went into labour last night, and delivered a male child at about 9pm. Sir, after the child was delivered her abdomen continued to remain distended and the midwife was unable to decide what should be done, so she didn't cut the cord. The family decided to bring her here. They travelled on a bullock cart, with the baby between her legs, still connected to the umbilical cord. They reached a couple of hours ago and, on seeing her state, I admitted her to the labour ward.

"We cut the cord and the first baby is absolutely fine. The second one was in transverse lie, and Maushi did internal version and corrected the position bi-manually, after which we started her on a Pitocin drip. She delivered a second baby boy after ten minutes on the drip and the placenta was delivered after half an hour of the baby's birth. The single placenta was having two umbilical cords.

"Both the identical babies have an APGAR of ten. Methergin has been given to the mother, and at present, she is resting."

"Arre, Anand, you did all this and didn't inform me?" Dr. Nisal was a tad annoyed.

"I'm sorry, Sir. Everything..... happened so fast...that I just carried on doing what had to be done."

"Come, let's go and see them." He got up to go.

We walked to the ward together. I was wondering what he had on his mind. He sounded angry with the fact that I went ahead and managed a complicated case all by myself without informing him. He didn't say it, but something was irking him and it was plainly evident from his demeanour, I decided to keep quiet and let the storm blow over.

At the bedside he examined the kids and agreed that both were normal. The mother, hitherto asleep, had awoken, sensing that someone was at her bedside. Dr. Nisal asked her how she was and she said that she was tired, very tired. He reassured her that everything was fine. And after this rather perfunctory examination we left the room. He said, "They seem alright. Have you given her an antibiotic?

"Yes, Sir."

"Okay," He started to walk towards his office and asked, "Anything else?"

"No, Sir."

"Okay."

"Thank you, Sir."

Knowing that all was well with the patient, I left for my room. There was this all-pervading sense of fulfilment and satisfaction of having done something worthwhile. I was really happy that this delivery concluded smoothly and, at the end of it all, both mother and sons were in good health. I was also very thankful for Maushi's support. In fact, my respect for her skill and wisdom jumped to an altogether new level. I reached the room reflecting again on my days at the Cama and Albless Hospital where we had learnt all our basics of obstetrics and gynaecology.

I remember telling Dr. Mrs. Kar, my unit head at Cama Hospital, that I would never take ob-gyn as my subject for specialisation even whilst knowing that I could be good at it. I had maintained that I was learning the subject and attending deliveries only so that I could, one day, give my family the best treatment when they needed it. The training that I underwent in Cama hospital was serving me well in this small town hospital. I was thanking, in my mind, all my mentors for bringing me to the level of competence that enabled me to handle these difficult situations. I was lost in my reveries when Dadan and Yogendra returned to the room.

"What are you thinking, Anand."

"I'm just thinking of how exciting this morning was. In two hours, so much happened."

"Really. It feels great when you do something challenging."

"Really... But, Dr. Nisal is annoyed with me....I think."

"He has no reason to be annoyed. You have done well," said Dadan surprised.

"I know, but still....I should have informed him. Maybe that was protocol. And I breached it."

"Never mind, yaar. Nothing went wrong, so don't fret." Yogendra said

"Not fretting. Just,....That pure joy of a job well done is diluted with this little tactical error."

"Come, let's eat"

"Let's eat."

61. In the News

The next morning, when we reached the OPD to commence our day's work, Sister Kadrekar, who was on duty then, came over looking very excited. She had a copy of the Kaal Nirnay, the local Marathi newspaper, in her hand. "Did you see this, doctor?" she asked, waving the newspaper at us. "Our boss is in the news."

Surprised, I took the newspaper from her hand and Dadan and I quickly scanned the first page. There, staring at us, was a picture of Paru seated cross-legged on the bed, with her twins on her lap, beaming from ear to ear, with Dr. Nisal by her side, looking very satisfied and circumspect.

The text of the article, in Marathi, was essentially proclaiming the story of Paru, making the trip from Wada to Jawhar, on a bullock cart, with her first born baby delivered and lying between her legs for the entire journey. Further, it went on to elaborate how Dr. Nisal had promptly cut the cord of the first baby, gone on to do the internal version of the second baby who was lying transversely in the womb, and thereafter, how he had delivered this child smoothly, and that now, both the boys and their mother were doing well. The article went on to say that the twins were born twelve hours apart, which was a kind of record of sorts. Maybe, for the first time in the history of Jawhar, twins had been delivered twelve hours apart after so much hardship and risk to the mother's well-being.

There was no mention of Maushi's efforts or for that matter, any other staff members efforts. There was no allusion to our contribution to this delivery. It was all about Dr. Nisal.

"This is ridiculous! Blatantly ridiculous! This is mean, wrong, and unfair." Dadan was livid with self-righteous indignation. He was black and white in his values, and this kind of misrepresentation of facts was beyond his comprehension and tolerance. Seeing his outburst, I actually forgot to get angry.

"Dadan, calm down. He knows, in his heart, what the truth is. Just forget it. He got his corner in the sky. Maybe he needed it. Good for him."

"What do you mean. He can't do this. He is blatantly lying! He has no right to do this."

"Dadan, hold on. He is the head of this hospital, so whatever happens here, is actually at his behest. Suppose we did something wrong, we wouldn't be in trouble, he would. So, if we do something good, the credit can go to him first. I do agree that he was not magnanimous enough to share the credit but, I guess, it is normal human nature. Forget it!"

Meanwhile, the newspaper article had a profound impact on the townspeople of Jawhar, and Paru had become a celebrity overnight. She was portrayed as the brave lady who weathered tremendous odds to make the trip to Jawhar in a bullock cart. She was the tenacious girl who could withstand so many hardships and she was the mother of two potential greats! ..and so on. She had several visitors coming in just to see her twins and to greet her.... and Dr. Nisal was basking in his new found popularity.

We showed the newspaper to Yogendra and his first reaction was of rage........ nothing less. He was livid with Dr. Nisal's having taken the credit for something he didn't even know was there. He ranted for a while, and then he calmed down and shrugged it off. None of us could hold a grudge for long. "Anand, Dadan, the twins are really cute. I was with them for a while. They are so sweet."

Boss took the credit for yesterday's case. It brought him a lot of fame and praise. What was he feeling in his own heart? It's something I'd like to know.

62. An Unexpected Visitor

Scarcely a week after Paru's news-making delivery, there was another very happy moment. Dadan was assisting Dr. Dhande with the vasectomies, whilst I was doing some dressings of patients' with foot ulcers, when suddenly, there was loud conversation and sounds of someone being greeted very warmly and effusively. I looked up from my vantage point, but saw nobody, the sounds of excited and animated conversations seemed to be coming from around the corner. I walked across the distance to the entrance foyer, and there, I saw all the staff of the hospital were gathered around somebody whom I couldn't see. I was curious to know who this was, who commanded such love and adulation. I walked up to the group and, as the nurses saw me approach, they made way for me. As they did so I saw who it was.

I couldn't believe my eyes at first. I thought maybe I was imagining what I saw. But no! There she was......As clear as day! It was Dhavali!

She was there in front of me, in flesh and blood, on her own feet, looking strong. She had a radiance on her skin which had an healthy sheen.

"Dhavali!!" I exclaimed, overjoyed to see her.

"Namaskar, Doctor! How are you?"

"Namaskar, Dhavali. I am fine and how are you? And where is Satya?"

"I am alright now. So much better than before."

"Chhaan...very good."

"Satya couldn't come. After leaving the hospital I took good care of myself, the wound healed gradually, and now I am completely alright. The wound is closed."

"Oh! That is wonderful news. Come in Dhavali. Let me see you properly."

I ushered her into the OPD and we all sat down around her. Dadan and Yogendra had also joined us. They were delighted to see her too. Dadan had been involved in her treatment as much as I had.

Everyone was dying to talk to her, and listen to her story, after she was discharged from the hospital. "Dhavali, saangh. Tell us your story, Dhavali. Tell us everything, from the time we sent you home till today. Everything!"

"Doctor, Sister, I was so happy to go home after so many days in the hospital. Satya and I reached very comfortably by bus." There was a gleem in her eyes when she said 'by bus'. She knew we would instantly remember that day when she had walked in the rain to reach us when she was so sick. "After reaching we settled down to our routine. Satya found himself some jobs on other farms where they paid him well. He was expected to work in the fields.

Whilst he was away for the day, I would do some light work on our farm. I chopped wood, piled it up, cut the grass which was quite overgrown by then, stacked the hay and did other odd jobs. I also put in the new crop of peanuts.

"I cleaned the house and applied a new coat of dung and mud on the floor and walls. I cooked and ate regularly. Doctor, every time I ate I remembered you because you had told me to eat well or else I would be very sick. I didn't want to be sick. I did all this work and kept busy because I didn't want to remember my bad times and the time when I was down. Our neighbours were very kind, and we would often sit together at the village well and talk. It felt good to have their support. One of the girls in the neighbourhood did my dressings for some days. Then one day I decided to leave it open and I was so happy to see that it started healing very fast. It took a month to heal but now it is closed completely." She was smiling broadly through this disclosure.

Dhavali not only looked well, she looked extremely happy. She was so much more positive. She had a sun-cooked look. I'm sure her haemoglobin must have improved as the sickly pallor had gone. Her abdominal examination showed the jagged scar which had now closed completely. There was no other abnormality I could find on her. She was well at last!

She had made this trip with two other women from her village. They wanted to visit some relatives in Jawhar. They were all going to return that evening. Dhavali's fleeting visit brought back memories of the rainy night in September when we first met. She was all but dead from exhaustion, malnutrition, and advanced pregnancy with twins. The risks we had taken to operate on her and the nightmarish events that followed sent a shudder down my spine. In the heat of that moment we made some extremely daring decisions and fortunately, we were able to help her come out of the troubled waters. The thought of her twins and our inability to save them, was still a source of immense regret and remorse. For a moment, I visualised this smiling girl, Dhavali, with her twins in her arms, and the sadness deepened. The twins would have been three months old and could have been a source of so much joy. But alas! That was not to be. Dhavali was not as fortunate as Paru, whose ordeal was so similar but the outcome so different.

The nurses were so engrossed with Dhavali, so animatedly hanging on to every word she was saying. Individually and collectively, the girls had spared no effort to help Dhavali recover from her terrible malady. This had forged a bond that was deep, as it was strong. Their love for this girl, and their sense of commitment and involvement in her progress to health, were etched in my mind as exemplary events in medical practice of the highest quality.

"Dhavali, ek photo!" She beamed with excitement and blushed despite her complexion which was the colour of dark chocolate. I bade them to wait whilst I hurried to the room to fetch my camera. This photo had a deep and sacred value for all of us. It was the symbol of a memory which has no parallel. Dhavali had come out of the blue, taught us many things, and would be gone soon. And here she was again, in front of us, seemingly like a full stop to a story. A story of grit, determination, bravado, intrigue, despair, sadness, grief, tenacity, resilience, innovation, adventure, commitment and love. Dhavali had, unwittingly, been a source of this extensive education and experience for all of us. Her coming into our lives, most certainly, left us as better people. The sun was past its peak when Dhavali and her friends prepared to leave to return home. She joined her hands in the traditional greeting and her eyes said a million things. She was going to return to her home and we would soon be back to our homes. This was a farewell of sorts......one of the 'forever' kinds. We still didn't know from where she came, and now she was about to leave for that unknown destination. She knew deep down inside, as we did too, that we would probably never meet again.

63. The Royal Summons

Hemant and Hiroo had come back. The five of us had just finished our morning routine when we received a message saying that there was a gentleman at the front gate wanting to meet me,

"Can't be me. Must be wanting to meet the Boss."

"No, Sir. He said he wants to meet you, Dr. Gokani."

"Go, Anand. See what he wants."

I rose to go and see who it was and what he wanted. On reaching the front of the hospital I was met by a middle-aged gentleman, who introduced himself as Mr. Pimpale. He further said that he was the personal assistant to the Maharaja of Jawhar, His Royal Highness Shri Digvijaysinh Mukne.

The Maharaja's palace is on the way to the Hanuman Temple and Sunset Point so we had often passed it by and secretly wished to see how beautiful it was from inside, but we never had the courage to venture inside the palace compound. And. now the Maharaja's personal assistant was here looking for me. I couldn't believe it at first and thought it was a prank. Of course, I was pleasantly surprised to see this gentleman and was keen to know what he wanted.

"Namaskar! What can I do for you? I am Dr. Anand Gokani."

Sir, Saheb's wife, Smt. Indiraraje Mukne is unwell and Saheb would like you to make a visit to the Palace to see her and advise her the treatment," he said. At first I was tongue-tied, surprised, overwhelmed! A moment later I composed myself and asked, "When?"

"When is it convenient to you?"

It was 2 pm and lunch was pending. I said, "Is 4 pm okay?"

"Okay, Sir. I'll send you the car at 3.45 pm." We bid each other farewell and I returned to the room.

As I entered, the others pounced on me and demanded to know what this was all about. "What happened. Tell us." They were keen to know what happened in this meeting. I told them of my impending meeting with the Maharaja and his wife at 4 pm. Having informed them, there was mayhem for the next ten minutes. Jibes, taunts, digs, and many sarcastic comments were issued by all of them. Teasing me of my newly acquired status.

"Ooh, big man....."

"Maharaja wants you!"

"Now you won't look at us..."

"Big league huh, Anand? Don't become too big."

And the jibes and digs continued while we ate lunch. I couldn't help smiling throughout lunch. Their comments, their miming, the mischief, was immensely amusing. Suddenly a thought occurred, that wiped the smile off my face.

"Hey, Anand. What happened. Why suddenly so serious?"

"Yaar, I'm going to the Palace to meet the Maharaja but....but I don't think I have any appropriate clothes to wear."

"Hahahaha! Dikhne mein Hero, pocket mein Zero!"

"Now what? You will have to present yourself well, you know."

"I'll manage with my simple stuff. Can't be helped. He wants me .....not my clothes. I still can't figure how he got my name. Maybe it's all a big mistake." I was a tad apprehensive about my attire as we had gotten used to utter simplicity in our present environment. In my wildest dreams I had never thought that I would be summoned to meet the Maharaja of Jawhar. Here I was....Going to meet him in an hour's time and still, far from ready.

"Take your stethoscope, Anand"

"Do you want a torch?"

"Pen?"

They wouldn't stop making fun of me. I left them to speculate why I was going. The car was there, waiting for me. A white Ambassador, with Mr. Pimpale and the chauffeur of the car waiting within. I was suddenly seized with a kind of apprehension. It was one thing to treat the Adivasis and quite another to treat the Rani Saheba. And what if it was something that I didn't understand? What if I fumbled or was hesitant in my approach. One after another, apprehensions of probable or possible blunders that could happen, crossed my mind and plagued my psyche. As we approached the Palace, I really wished I could have been closer to the secure environs of the quarters of the cottage hospital. My trepidation mounted as we approached the Palace.

Finally we reached the gates from where there was a long driveway, lined by trees, leading to the Palace. The driveway was bumpy, but as we reached the porch, the road gave way to a tiled flooring, which lead to the main porch. I alighted at the porch from where I was escorted to the main living room. Shri Digvijaysinh Mukne, was waiting there to receive me. He was a very tall gentleman, with a stately demeanour and good-natured eyes. He had a welcoming smile as we shook hands warmly.

He started the conversation,"Thank you for coming."

"It's my pleasure. I am indeed privileged to be here," I said with a smile.

We went inside the living room and settled down there. "My wife has been unwell for a while and we don't know what to do," he started saying. With a concerned look on his face, he continued," We are very worried about her. Her sister, Sarladevi Chowgule, is your mother's good friend in Bombay. She told us that you were here and that you could help to treat her."

"Where is she?" I asked.

"She is resting inside. Let me give you her history before we go inside."

"Sure," I said. Now I understood how I landed this royal invitation.

"Indira has been unwell since some days. She has been having persistent cramps in the abdomen, and loose motions since about ten days and as a result she has become very weak. She has lost some weight too. We tried several doctors and many remedies. I am worried now. Sarladevi told me that you were very good and would be able to help me with her problem. My assistant, Pimpale, tells me that people in the town speak well about you. They say that you have helped so many seriously ill patients to get well. Please have a look at her and tell me what i should do next,"

All along this conversation I was smiling. I couldn't help feel great with all the praise being heaped on me. Of course I was taking the collective credit for work done by all of us. Nevertheless, it felt good to hear praise.

"May I ask you some questions please?"

"Yes, sure? Ask whatever you need to know"

"Does she have......." and I ran through the entire checklist of symptoms and causative factors of abdominal problems. After I was done with the history I asked if I could see her. In my mind I was reaching a conclusion which I needed to confirm by examination.

I was ushered into a room where Her Royal Highness was resting. I greeted her and asked, "How are you Ma'am?"

"Not too well," she said. "I have this cramping pain that keeps coming up time and again......" she related all her problems and I listened attentively. Although I had already heard her history from her husband, I still listened, hoping for a new lead which the patient herself may afford me. Listening was an art, stressed by our teachers, and was the most important tool in the quest to help patients get better.

After she had finished, I asked her if she had done any tests. None, they had said.

"May we get a stool test and a complete blood count, please? It would help immensely to give her the appropriate medications." "We can get them done."

"Very well. As soon as we have the reports I will give her the treatment."

"I'll have these tests done at Thane today and possibly have the reports by tomorrow morning. We can meet again tomorrow and take the matter forward."

"Yes. We can meet tomorrow evening. At 6pm?"

"Perfect. Doctor, why don't you have dinner with us tomorrow. It would be a pleasure to have you over for dinner."

"Sir, not tomorrow. I will certainly come again for dinner when she is well and can eat with us. Thank you for your invitation though."

"Okay. Six tomorrow. Doctor what are your fees?" The question surprised me. He had offered in good faith, but as interns, we were not entitled to take fees or do any sort of private practice.

His gesture touched me, "Sir, we are interns and are not entitled to fees and not allowed private practice. So there are no fees. My visit and consult are purely a friendly gesture and I am delighted for the opportunity."

"Okay. We meet tomorrow. My car will drop you to your hospital."

"Thank you. It was a pleasure meeting you."

"Indeed, likewise. I look forward to seeing you tomorrow. Good bye."

I returned to the hospital in the Maharaja's car. At the door of our quarters the hawks were waiting for me. No sooner I reached, they pounced on me, saying, "What happened? Tell us!"

"Oh! It was nice. The Maharaja is a nice man. Unassuming and dignified. His wife is unwell so he called me to see her. I'm going tomorrow to see them again, I asked for a CBC and routine stool, reports should be back by then."

"Bas! Now you are a lost case. You won't have time for us! You have become a big league doctor."

"Arre, no, yaar. Nothing like that. One visit to the Palace and you think I've become big? Nothing like that! I am the same. Never will change."

We discussed random things whilst waiting for dinner to be served. The days were short and climate cold. After sunset a kind of gloom set in, which had a kind of soporific effect which made you want to just get into bed under the rugs and sleep.

64. The Rani Saheba

The morning after was cold with a thick mist pervading outside the house. It was an ordeal to get out of bed. The temperature had dropped suddenly and the effects of winter were all too evident. We had no heating device in our room so the room was chilled.

Vahini was knocking on the door but none of us was yet out of our beds. I wrapped the blanket around my head and shoulders tightly and got out of bed to let her in. A hot cup of tea would redeem this situation. Some sunlight would be more than welcome.

Vahini was wrapped up in a thick shawl, just as I was, and she looked cold. She was shivering outside but she was brave and had put her act together despite the cold, to come and make our breakfast and tea. She got the stove going and had tea ready for us in a few minutes. The others also rolled out of bed one by one. Wrapped in blankets, we all headed to the anteroom, where the gentle morning sun was streaming in to give us the much needed warmth. Even the blankets were seemingly inadequate today.

We had a normal routine day. There was a lot of work but nothing challenging. The day wore on and, before I realised, it was 6 pm and the Maharaja's vehicle had arrived to pick me up. The same trepidation seized me. Being so used to the security of routine work, this specialised work of meeting a celebrity at his own terms was a daunting prospect....and every new experience is filled with potential apprehensions. I arrived at the Palace in the same state. At the door, I was greeted by the Maharaja's son, Mahendrasinh Mukne, a tall, lean and athletic young man, 17 years of age. He looked every bit the Royal Prince or Yuvraj. He greeted me warmly and took me straight to his mother's room where his father, His Royal Highness, was waiting for us.

"Hello doctor, thank you for coming."

"You are most welcome," I said, and then looking towards Rani Saheba, I asked, "How are you today?"

"The test results have arrived, doctor," he said, handing me the papers.

I looked at the reports carefully. The stool test showed mucus, blood and the presence of entamoeba histolytica, the parasite causing her symptoms. The complete blood count showed a normal haemoglobin, a slightly raised white cell count, with an increase in the eosinophils. Put together, this confirmed the diagnosis of chronic amoebiasis.

"Madame, as I had suspected, there is an infection in your colon that is causing the symptoms. The cause is evident in the test. I will give you some treatment for 14 days and you will be immensely better. You must also make some changes in your food so that you don't get this infection again. No more eating food from outside, especially food from road-side stalls." I said the last sentence with a broad smile, knowing full well how the Rani Saheba loved to indulge in street food like chaat and pani puri.

There was a sheepish look on her face and she broke into an embarrassed smile. "Doctor, I love chaat. I had it every day for some days. There is a vendor who sells it near our home in Poona. Do you think that could have been the cause?"

"I can't discount that possibility. In fact, the likelihood is pretty high." I said, putting aside dogma and choosing diplomacy. Human weaknesses don't exempt any class or creed of people and the same weaknesses are our prime susceptibilities. Whether prince or pauper, one can get the same disease. I wrote the treatment for her and explained the dosage, precautions and side-effects.

"Doctor, yesterday you went off in a hurry. You never had anything to eat or drink. Please stay today and have dinner with us."

The invitation was so affectionate, and so difficult to refuse, but I sincerely felt that if I settle down to have dinner with them, when Rani Saheba is unwell, it would not look good. I thought it would be better to wait till her health was good and then to rightfully capitalise the invitation. I said to them, "Thank you so much for your kind invitation. I am, indeed, touched. However, I feel it won't be right since you are unwell. Why don't we meet for dinner when you are completely well and can enjoy the same with us?"

Rani Saheba, looked disappointed but she understood my sentiment. She said, "Okay, let's fix the date today. Shall we meet after exactly two weeks from today? The course should be over by then, I hope I will be better too, and you will come to see me again."

I relented to her warm and kind invitation saying,"Okay, surely, we will all eat together on that day."

After that, we bid each other farewell and I headed for the hospital in their car. The second visit had given me a deeper insight into their nature and temperament. Earlier, I was overwhelmed by the thought of seeing the Maharaja. I was filled with trepidation, apprehension and a degree of fear. We were used to dealing with simple folk who didn't have a voice. We were their voice. We were the giants amongst them. But this situation was different. I was going to see someone who had a voice, an opinion and was possibly, wiser and more experienced than I was. This prejudicial thought was my prime pitfall. The cause of my discomfiture was this preconceived notion that they were superior to me and therefore it would be difficult for me to assert myself before them. All these negative feelings took root in my own mind, created by me, and they went on to cause me untold distress. Whereas, in actuality, they were the most wonderfully down-to-earth people who respected me for what I was. Their simplicity and warmth was disarming and winning from the word go. My second visit allayed all my fears and put me to great ease. They were the same as all of us, they felt the same pain, they had the same fears, and the same misconceptions and the same human frailties. I was so relieved by this revelation and it permitted me the confidence to give off my best to them. I realised that the mind itself was the cause of all our abilities and disabilities. We personally ensure our failure by playing up to our negative thought processes and entertaining them.

I left the Palace exhilarated and happy. I was, in fact, looking forward to meeting them again. I sensed the beginning of a deep and abiding friendship.

65. Loose Ends

The days work was over, and we were all sitting together in the late evening, in the area just outside our quarters. The sun was going down and the light was dimming to the hues of twilight.

We had been discussing our ward patients and sharing details of the interesting episodes that each one of us had experienced whilst treating them. I suddenly remembered the patient with the foot ulcer. "Yogi, what happened to Shankar, that guy with the foot ulcer. Soon after you made that window in the plaster I left for Bombay. Any progress thereafter, any diagnosis?"

"Of course! He had a terrible neuropathy. No sensation in the foot up to mid shin level. And because he didn't have diabetes I thought it could have been 'H'. His ESR was 98 mm at the end of 1 hour. I sent him to Thane for a biopsy. That would clinch the issue, I thought."

"Yes of course. I think it must be Hansen's disease. He had neuropathy, wasting of his palms and loss of sensation, his facial hair was scanty and he had a somewhat leonine face. Typical of Hansen's disease. Did you feel his nerves?"

"Not consciously....means ...I didn't look for them."

"Yogi, yaar, I'm convinced it was 'H'. When is he coming back with the biopsy report? Would love to see him again and start his treatment. Should have got him on the first shot. Shouldn't have bunked Dr. Dongre's classes. If we had attended then we wouldn't have missed this. I thought Jopling was more than enough so I freely bunked skin and leprosy clinics. I know the theory but the practical exposure would have helped so much."

"Never mind, yaar."

"Hey!" Hiroo interjected. "I heard Dhavali had come back? Anand you never told us."

"Oh! Yes, yes." I exclaimed. "She had come and she looked great. Her wound had healed completely."

"Wow! It closed?!" Hiroo exclaimed, full of curiosity for more info. "How? Only dressings?"

"You know, Hiroo. When I was in Bombay I was thinking of her case once. I was so uncomfortable sending her with the open wound. She was just adamant to go! She said that, at home, she just did the dressings and kept the wound clean."

"You know what, boss," Hiroo said, "I think when all that pus was coming out and we were doing dressings daily, the Shirodkar's suture must be getting disintegrated inside and bits and pieces may be coming out with the pus and we didn't notice the pieces. That's the only way I think she could have healed. Some bits must have gone with the lochia and some with the pus from the wound. Can't say."

"Indeed, an intriguing case she was."

"I still feel bad about loosing the kids. Could we have done something differently?" I mused. "Anything at all?"

"Given the circumstances, I think we did pretty well. Can't be everywhere and do everything right, can we?" said Hiroo consolingly.

Vahini had just arrived to make our dinner. On seeing her I suddenly felt the pangs of hunger. I think we were all hungry.

"Talking of dinner, shall we have a farewell dinner for our bosses. It would be great fun!"

"Hey, that's a brilliant idea. How do you say we go about it?"

"It's just an idea, just now it dawned on me."

"We can make the food too. Ourselves." Dadan said with mischief in his eyes.

After a longish pause, Hiroo said, "Let's all make one thing. I'll do the salad. Anand, what will you make? Hemant? And you, Dadan, Yogi?"

Hemant said, "I'll make the soup."

Yogi, "I'll get the plates and cutlery. Beg, borrow or steal."

I said, "I'll make bread and cheese pakoras!"

"Hahaha! Anand, the most complicated thing you will make? Or will you ask Vahini to make?" Hiroo chided.

"What do you mean? Of course, I'll make it."

"Achha! Let's see."

"Dadan, you are responsible for the most important dish! Biryani and raita. Vegetarian or mutton?"

"We will keep it veg only. Everybody enjoys then." Dadan said.

"No, yaar!"

"Okay chal. I'll take Vahini's help and make both. Some mutton and some veg."

"So when shall we have it?"

"Let's see.....hmm.," ....thinking aloud...."Today is Tuesday. Let's do Friday."

"Friday?" Looking around for approval.

"Yes!"

"Okay, Friday 8 pm."

"Who are we calling?"

"Everyone, no? That is, Drs. Dhande, Nisal, Ujwala and all the nurses and......Bas."

"Okay, done."

"From tomorrow we have to dish out the invites. Whoever meets whoever! Tell them."

So, we have a new project to handle now. Project Party!

66. The Party

Every moment of the next two days was spent in planning our rag tag party. We were all amateurs in this field yet we wanted to make a big impression, so whenever something occurred to us we were keen on sharing it with each other. Slowly and steadily the party was taking shape.

"How much money are we going to need for this party?"

Hiroo said, "I made a rough calculation and think about 600 rupees would suffice."

We had that in the kitty (read treasury) so there was no need to search further. Hiroo and Hemant did the shopping and all stocks were ready for use. Early on Friday morning I woke up to do my bit. It was six in the morning and the weather was cold.

"Hell, why do I get myself into these situations? It's so much easier to just sleep in bed, wrapped in blankets." Reluctantly, I pushed the blankets away and got up. I wished Vahini was here to make me a cup of tea but that seemed a faraway dream presently. I splashed some cold water on my face to wake up fully. and it did the trick in possibly the most cruel way.

After duly washing up I set about my kitchen project. I had the next one and a half hours to finish what I needed to do and then routine would start. I opened the Amul cheese tin and took the entire block of cheese from it. I had to grate the entire block into a vessel, to which i was going to add, some chopped onions, coriander and green chillies. Having prepped this mix, I manually kneaded the entire mix into a mushy paste. The next step was to prepare the bread. I flattened each slice of bread after first soaking and then pressing the slice in a flat plate. Having flattened the bread I put the cheese mix on it and wrapped the bread around it, patting it into the shape of a sausage. I did this fifty times over and just as I was on the last one Vahini walked in. I was so engrossed in my work that I didn't notice the arrival of sunlight, the knock on the door and Vahini's entry into the pantry. I was suddenly brought back to reality when she came in. She started laughing when she saw me doing what I was doing.

"Arre, doctor. You are cooking? You go treat patients. I'll do this. This is not your place," she laughed and made to push me out of the pantry.

"Just finished, Vahini!" I said, pointing to the neat array of cheese pakoras in the steel plate. "Now you have to fry them at night."

She placed them on a moist cloth and put them into a steel box. "They will stay well in this cold climate. Now you go and sit and I will make tea."

"Okay." I left the pantry satisfied with my work. My job was done. In the afternoon Dadan and Vahini would make the biryani and raita. And the rest will be just before dinner. Sorted.

The day went well. Any amount of work was possible in the cold climate as there never was a trace of fatigue. Preparations continued as the day wore on and by 6 pm we were all set. We spent the next hour tinkering about in our little abode. Making sure that everything was ready.

At 8 pm sharp Dr. and Mrs. Nisal walked in. Soon to be followed by Dr. Dhande and Dr. Ujwala. The nurses had to wind up their shifts, and make sure all the patients were taken care of, their medications given and their notes updated. They came in by 8.30 pm. We were now in full strength and the party was warming up.

"Ma'am, look. Your painting has been up on this wall since we have been here."

"Arre, I didn't even notice it. I had given it to a doctor from your college three years ago."

"Do you remember his name, Ma'am?"

"No. Too long ago."

"So, Ma'am, in a short while after we go, you will forget us also?" Dadan asked her with the obvious intent of teasing her.

Pat came the reply, "Maybe." As earlier alluded to, Dr. Ujwala was easy prey for the mischievous, but she was, in her own inimitable style, able to hold her own, despite the odds being stacked against her. But this banter was without malice and in a lighter vein.

"So!" Dr. Nisal exclaimed. It was like he was going to say something. "So, boys! Your term is almost coming to an end."

"Yes, Sir. We are painfully aware of the passage of these last few days."

"Never mind boys, this is life. Time moves on and on. The scene changes again and again. And with every scene there is adjustment, adaptation, and that's how you get experience. The more experience you get, the more you are valued by the world. So don't worry. I'm sure you all will do very well."

Dr. Nisal placed a hand on Dadan's shoulder benevolently, and asked, "Dadan, what are you going to do after finishing this internship."

"Uncertain, Sir. I haven't got the best marks."

"Didn't get the best marks? Then you will be the most successful. Marks are not important for success and happiness."

Dr. Dhande added, "Those who got good marks got stuck and those who didn't, explored the world and got more experience and became very successful.

"Really," Dr. Ujwala chimed in, "I agree."

"Sir, then why does everyone run for marks and positions and postings and degrees?"

"Some are ordained to stay in one place and learn and some have to move from place to place to learn. Both have their downsides and their upsides. As you move on in life you will realise."

"Achha, Hiroo. What are you planning to do?"

"Sir, I want to join the Indian Armed Forces. I want to be a surgeon in the army."

"Wow! That's so good." The nurses all gave him a short, spontaneous applause. They had remained very quiet till now, ostensibly due to Sir's presence, but on hearing Hiroo's noble desire, they couldn't resist an inpromptu expression of their approval and appreciation.

"So, Hiroo, Jawhar must have given you a superb, well-rounded experience."

"Indeed, it did, Sir. I enjoyed myself here and, in the bargain, learnt a lot too."

"Hahaha. Sir, he also learnt how to bargain here. He is the best to get a good deal in the vegetable market."

"Hahaha. I think that is a bigger lesson in life. the art of living well within our means. Indeed, Hiroo, then you will definitely go very far in life."

Vahini had just brought out the soup and Hemant was helping her serve it. She had also fried the cheese pakoras to a lovely golden colour. She carried them in a tray so that everyone could help themselves. Dr. Dhande picked up the first piece and, dipping it in some mint chutney, bit into it. "This is very tasty. Who made it?"

I was smiling but didn't say anything. Dadan said, "Anand made them."

"Hmmm. You know something about cooking also. New dimension." Dr. Nisal said. Everyone liked them and were appreciative. The soup, too, was wonderful in this climate....Tangy and hot!

"Anand, what are your plans?"

"Sir, plans are plenty. But don't know whether I will get what I want next term.

"Why? Why are you sounding negative, Anand? You are normally so positive!"

"Just....Sir, my immediate fate depends on so many people's choices that I do sometimes despair. My heartfelt wish is to do an MD in General Medicine. There are only eight seats and I am fourteenth on the list. If six people ahead of me take something else then I will get the last seat. That is my only hope."

"Don't worry, Anand. Have faith in God. You will get what you want. Just watch."

"Yes, Sir. I'm living in faith, because what had to be done I have done. Now it's faith and hope!"

"Dinner is ready!" Vahini announced and brought out the vessels with the food to the table in the ante room. Our discussion had gone on for a good one hour and we were all hungry. "Please take."

Leaving us to eat, she left for a quick visit to her home to have dinner with her family.

We all loaded our plates with biryani, raita and salad. The light banter generally centred around questions on our future plans. Yogendra said he wanted surgery and Hemant was keen on general practice. The discussion and dinner moved at a comfortable pace. The food had turned out better than we expected and it was heartening to see the girls take generous helpings for a change. There was an animated conversation on flow, breaking the silence of an otherwise peaceful night.

Peels of laughter, loud voices, and a happy camaraderie supervened at the quarters. There was a sense of satisfaction as the party had shaped better than we had expected. It was close to midnight when they all left.

We spent the next hour cleaning the mess in the quarters. We stacked the dishes and the utensils to be washed in the morrow, mopped the floor, and tidied the beds so that we could sleep in a clean room. Tired, but fulfilled, we crept into bed and under the rugs, but the conversation continued from the safe confines of our netted cubby holes till, one by one, we drifted off to sleep.

67. Dinner at the Palace

A new morning, the beginning of the last week in Jawhar. A shadow of apprehension rising insidiously in the mind's background. A nagging fear. It felt like the clock had taken the full circle and had come to rest at the same spot where we were when we first came to Jawhar. It was the same feeling of a looming uncertainty, insecurity, confusion. Ward rounds were light and clinic was routine. Fortunately so, because our minds were preoccupied by future events. Our meal was a scene of anxious discussion of the impending distribution of postings. Someone wanted surgery, someone medicine, some were readying for general practice but confidence levels were low. These thoughts kept weighing heavy on the mind.

What we wanted was crystal clear and not the source of stress. The stress was whether we would get what we wanted to do or not. That was the stress eating into our peace of mind and try as we would, it could not be quelled. A niggling fear of the unknown that kept irritating from within. Will I get the right posting? Will I get a good teacher as a guide? Will I be able to cope with the pressures of post-graduate medical education? Of the latter I had no doubts. I had already been tested comprehensively in Jawhar. I knew that hard work was not a deterrent to me. A few more days of uncertainty. Then the interviews and after the interviews everything would be crystal clear. I tried hard to push this problem and these thoughts out of my mind.

"Anand, there is someone to meet you at the door."

Wondering who it could be, I made my way from the clinic to the front foyer. "Oh, Mr. Pimpale! How are you?" Seeing him, I remembered that I had started Rani Saheba on the treatment two weeks ago and it was now time to meet her. Mr. Pimpale had probably come to remind me.

"Doctor, Rani Saheba, wants to know if you can visit her this evening. She has also asked if you could stay and have dinner with them."

"What time shall I come?"

"May I come and pick you up at 7.30 pm tonight?"

"That should be fine. I'll be ready."

Back in the room, "Who was that, Anand?"

"The Maharaja's PA." I said smugly. Just to incite some jealousy. A little cocky maybe. I was just dying to break the news to my friends that I was going to have dinner with the Maharaja's family tonight. "Guys, I'm out for dinner today"

"Now he will start bragging all over again. Oh I dined with the Maharaja. The plates were silver. The food was outstanding,...and .....and .....and. we won't hear the end of his royal adventures."

I looked at my friends, looking at me with mixed feelings....as if, saying, "Why can't you just see her and come back. Why dinner?" I heard the unspoken message loud and clear. "Okay, I'll see her and come back."

The day went by and soon it was time to go. The Palace car was waiting for me at 7.30pm. In ten minutes I was at the Palace. Now I was quite familiar with the Palace. The car pulled up in front of the main doorway and the guard opened the door. I stepped out just as Mahendrasinh, His Royal Highness' son appeared at the doorway to receive me.

"Welcome, doctor! We were just waiting for you to come."

"Thank you. How is Mummy?"

"She is much better, doctor. She is very happy."

"Oh, I'm so glad. Shall we meet her."

"Come right in."

We made our way to the living room where they were seated. I greeted them and took a seat. Rani Sahiba was looking much better. When we had met last she had been in bed and in pain. She had gained some weight in the last two weeks and looked fuller and happier. She had finished her course of antibiotics and presently was on no medications. After the questions on her health and the perfunctory medical examination were done we shifted to the lawn outside. It was pleasant and the garden looked lovely at twilight. Rani Saheba was now completely alright and that gave me a sense of satisfaction and boosted my confidence.

"Doctor, would you like a drink? We are expecting a friend to join us, so whilst we wait we can have a drink or two, if you like."

This question caught me off guard. During the undergraduate days we had our share of wild capers and I can't really claim innocence from the habits of vice. However, here in Jawhar, we had never indulged in tobacco or alcohol. In fact, we had never even thought of it. Our work kept us busy, and the company was stimulating and there was never any free time to allow our minds to wander from the straight and narrow path.

"Doctor, what would you like to drink?"

The question brought me back from my rumination and I stuttered a reply," Uh-huh,...anything really. Whatever you are having."

"Okay, shall we have some whiskey? Would you like it with soda or with water?"

"Hmmm........ I think I'll have it with soda, thank you." I said this, remembering my first foray with whiskey in college, when I had tried to be a daredevil and said I'd have mine 'on the rocks' and proceeded to polish off five large drinks, only to severely regret the consequences thereafter.

He poured me what looked like a large peg and the same for himself. The soda followed and then the clink of an ice cube. "Here we are. Your drink, doctor."

"Cheers!"

I picked up my glass, "Cheers."

The evening wore on, the journalist friend arrived, and, with him, came a million anecdotes on a wide array of subjects. Journalists are always privy to first hand news and we were treated to a feast of stories this evening. Intrigue, scandal, news, politics, analysis, gossip and so many other issues were brought out as if from some magic bag, and laid bare before this attentive audience who hung on to every word. The conversation carried on animatedly and time raced on. I forgot completely, my promise to my friends, of returning soon after I finished seeing Rani Saheba. Lost in this stream of interesting and exciting conversation, we didn't realise when it was midnight.

"My word! It's midnight! Didn't know where time ran away."

"Never mind, doctor. Do you have work pending?"

"No. Not really. My friends are all there and maybe they are worrying about me." I lied, knowing full well that they must have slept."

"Doctor, the dinner is ready. Shall we go inside?"

We rose and made our way inside to the magnificent dining room. The aroma of freshly cooked food accosted us as soon as we entered the dining room. Truly, it was a feast fit for kings. The dinner progressed amidst animated conversation, lucid humour and camaraderie. We were done by 1.30 am. It was time for farewells soon after. It had been a truly magnificent evening and I was sure that I was not going to forget how much I had enjoyed the company and hospitality. We parted with the promise of keeping in touch and meeting again. I informed Rani Saheba that I would be leaving Jawhar in a few days, and she was welcome to keep in touch even whilst I was in Mumbai. She wished me well and promised to keep in touch.

When I reached the quarters, everyone was asleep. In a few moments of changing, I was lost to the world too. The day's fatigue, topped by the gentle soporific effect of whiskey, topped by a superb meal was conducive to the best sleep ever.

68. A Small Crisis

The last few days of being in Jawhar were being spent in saying our farewells to those who we met frequently and may not meet again for a while. We met the vegetable and fruit vendors in the market, and the grocer, who we often frequented for all our petty needs, many patients and their families, the nurses' homes to meet their families, Krishnabhau, and some more townspeople, the love and affection we received from all these people was heart warming.

Amidst all this sentimental stuff there came a small crisis that needed resolution.

"Doctor, Nisal Saheb wants you in his office," said Mukne, who had come to the quarters to call me.

"Yes, I'll be there in a moment."......Why does he want me? A fleeting apprehension crossed my mind. Now what did I do?

I knocked on his door and entered. "Good morning, Sir. You called me?"

"Yes, Anand. Please sit down." He had some papers in front of him and he seemed a tad hesitant to say what he wanted to. "It's like this, Anand. I was just signing the completion certificates and I realised that you have not completed the stipulated time as per my records." He shuffled his papers on the table as if to buy time and frame his next moment better. "You were absent for the first two months of the term and the Dean's office had issued a telegram to inform you of the same.

And suddenly, the old skeleton which had been buried four months ago was exhumed and was about to haunt me all over again. I didn't respond, waiting for him to continue. My gut was in a cramp and suddenly, I had that horrible feeling of an impending disaster. My mind was feverishly thinking,. Now what is he going to say?....what if he denies me a certificate?....what will happen to the post-graduation posting interview early next month?......I wouldn't be eligible for that....I would have to wait six months for the next attempt. A hundred thoughts were racing through my head even as I waited for him to make the next statement.

"I can't waive off two months leave even if you have worked diligently. What I could do for you is grant you the allowable leave of four weeks, and reduce the period of absence to one month." "But, Sir, my interview for PG is on 7th of February. If I don't have my internship completion certificate then I won't qualify for it." I was dismayed! Not another road block in my life! Why! Why is everything so trying!? Why is everything so challenging?

My feelings must have been amply visible on my face. Dr. Nisal probably had a full view of my mind as it reflected in my demeanour. He seemed to be examining a thought carefully in his mind too.

"Okay, Anand, I have suggestion. I will exempt you from two weeks work but the remaining two weeks you will have to work. That means your term ends on the 30th of January. That will give you a week before your PG interviews. Is that alright?"

It was as if a large, dark cloud suddenly shifted and the sky was once again blue and bright. "Sir, that is so kind of you. I can do that...."My voice trailed off as I remembered that the new batch of interns would be arriving and they would be needing the quarters. Where would I live for the two weeks during which I was expected to work. "But.....Sir....The new interns?" I was thinking of a solution to my problem and was wondering if I should say it out aloud.

"What about them, Anand?"

"Sir, they will be coming and will be needing the doctors' quarters."

"Hmmmm,...... That's true." He was thinking again...and so was I.

He spoke first, "Okay, I understand. Let it be. What I will do is the following....You give me a leave application for one month. I will, on my part, exempt you from work for two weeks, and as for the remaining two weeks. you may return to Bombay and come back on the 30th of January for your completion certificate. That will take care of everything." So saying, he pushed the papers aside, dismissing the matter decisively.

I couldn't believe my luck. This was such a huge favour from him. My mood changed. "Sir, I can't thank you enough. It's, indeed, so kind of you!"

"Anand, I know that you have worked selflessly and diligently. I have watched you all very closely for the past four months and I know that you boys are sincere and hard working. The least I can do is to recognise your efforts and to help you along your paths." He smiled and added. "Anand, we are here to guide you, help you, and shape you for the future. We are not tyrants as we are portrayed by some people.

"We have also been students, and we have also faced the same trials and challenges that you are presently facing. We fully understand your apprehensions and anxieties." He paused for a moment, overcome by nostalgia and emotion. "Anand, we also had dreams for our future. Some of them we were able to realise, but some dreams we had to let go of, because circumstances didn't permit us to move on. Life doesn't let you do what you want and many-a-times you have to settle for what you have." He again paused, choosing and weighing his words.

"When i was young, I had so many dreams, but unfortunately my circumstances changed and I had to abandon my dreams and take up this government job. It's not that I chose this life by my free will. I had to take it up as a support for the many that depended on me. But now I have no regrets. I feel my dreams get realised when I see my students doing well in life. It's a joy that I can't put in words.... The joy of seeing your student shine, and do well and realise his ambitions. It's a surrogate joy, of realising our own unfulfilled dreams through someone else and knowing that you had a role, albeit a small one, in the achievements of your students. One day, when you will be a father you will remember and understand what I am saying today. I hope you will remember me then."

I could see what he meant, but not completely. At that moment I was simply trying to contain my joy at being let off the hook and being able to make it, unscathed, to the PG interview. I said, "Sir, thank you very much. I will never forget what you have taught me. I won't let you down. Sir, I am grateful to you for all that you have done for me and my colleagues."

He smiled and said,"Go. You must be having work to do."

I returned to my colleagues and told them everything that had transpired in the CMO's office. They listened with rapt attention. A new respect dawning in their minds for him as a teacher, as a doctor, as a human being. Suddenly we were being made aware of his humane and compassionate side. This little learning was to grow over the years to a kind of realisation.

69. One Last Time

As a sentimental keepsake we decided to visit the dam once more for one last visit. The day was bright, though cold and there was very little work at the hospital. The walk to the dam was exhilarating as always. This may have been the first time when we were visiting the dam in the early evening when the sun was up and bright. The sun was warm on the skin yet there was a cool breeze. A very happy mix of conditions.

"Guys, our internship is almost done and we all will be lost in our own worlds very soon. How time has flown past...!"

"Are you sad that we have to return to Bombay?"

Yes, I am sad. I am sad that our term is over, that we will all be following our separate paths, that we will be faced with so many uncertainties in our lives henceforth, and that we may not meet for years after this. I am sad. Indeed, I am sad.

Silence......save the lapping of the gentle waves on the surface of the lake and the soft hush of the breeze rustling the leaves. Everything was still. Yet there was turbulence in our minds. A defiant turbulence that challenged all logic and reason. An unrest that stole the peace and left the mind disquieted and restive.

Winter had set in and the cold air had a kind of freshness that was invigorating.The fragrance from wild flowers and the earthy smell of leaves lent a charm beyond description. And soon....all this would be behind us. We would be back to the ruthless grindstone in Bombay. To the noise, the dust, the crowds, the impersonal relationships, to the endless stream of sick humanity at the JJ Hospital with whom we would be spending the next three years.

The four months that had just gone by had been a tryst with destiny. Not very long ago I had wrestled with the dilemma of taking a light job versus taking a job that demanded my all......my wits, my logic, my heart, my soul, and the last drop of my physical energy. Did I ever regret my choice?

Regret? No way! My feelings were not remotely near regret. Frankly, my heart, presently, was in the throes of severe separation anxiety. Even as I did look forward to the post-graduate term going to commence next month, I still had a pang of longing that wanted me to stay here and continue to work for the welfare of the village folk. On that fateful afternoon, the revelations and the visions of the months gone by were crystal clear and in such vivid detail. Every patient, every incident, every conversation, every agonising detail came alive in the mind's eye and suddenly the permanence, or rather, the impermanence of existence took on a clearer picture. Generations of doctors before me had come and the future generations after me would also come to this place and seemingly do their best. People would come and people would go and so life will go on. Maybe the lot of the Adivasis would change for the better, maybe not. I realised that, presently, I could only do my bit and move on. However the altruist inside me kept on wondering what would become of the patients whom we had hitherto looked after. They would want a familiar face to see when they arrived at the hospital. What would they think, when they arrived and found that we were not there anymore, and that they were confronted with new doctors. Would they feel let down, would they be disappointed, would they feel betrayed or would they just continue as though nothing had changed?

These and a million other thoughts churned inside my mind.... and, sitting in the calming presence of the lake, lost in natural beauty and deep in thought, we remained there till the sun was about to set. We all realised that in a few days our lives were going to change drastically. There was a twinge of remorse and a lot of apprehension.

"It's late guys, don't you want to go home?

"Let's turn back. It's late and it's cold." I realised painfully that my light cotton shirt is not enough to protect me from the cold. I stood up from my seat on the ledge, thrust my hands resolutely into my trouser pockets and began to walk homewards. The others followed. A shiver ran down my spine. It was getting very cold and, in the last three days, the nip had changed to a bite. I picked up speed to keep warm but...to no avail.

"Hurry guys! This cold is getting to my bones."

"Ya, walk fast."

The walk back, in contrast to the rest of the afternoon, was made in silence. The cold outside and fires raging inside.

Understandably......Where would we be tomorrow? Another place, another job, other people, other responsibilities....a completely new world of experiences.

70. Parting Blues

As we approached the day of departure, the nurses, the staff, the regular patients all had something to say to us. It was as difficult for them as it was for us to express the feelings that seemed to well up within.

As the day drew to a close we repaired to the room for dinner. Vahini was in the kitchen, cooking. The aroma in the room was enticing, and we were hungry. We all sat down waiting for Vahini to bring out the dinner. She was silent today. There was an uncanny silence amongst us too. Normally when we were together there was always something to discuss. Some incident, some blunder, some case, some anecdote......just about anything! There was always something worth sharing. Today was no different.

There was enough to share but what we had on our minds was weighing heavy and today's sharing was best done in silence.

It was the last dinner in Jawhar today and we were all aware of it. Tomorrow we will be back in Bombay and dining at home with our families. Our packed bags were lined up neatly in the anteroom.

The atmosphere in the home was melancholy and sad.

"Vahini. Why so quiet? What's the matter?"

"Nothing. Just....," she said, leaving her sentence unfinished as her voice trailed off. We looked at each other, understanding perfectly what she was thinking and feeling. She averted our eyes as she brought out the food and placed it on the table. "It smells superb, Vahini. Kaay banavla aahe? What have you cooked today?" With a sheepish smile and a hint of a blush she replied, "Chicken curry, rice and vegetables. There are some chopped onions and pickled lemon in that," pointing her finger at the covered dish. "Do you want Oakbai's papads? There are some left."

"Yeah, sure. Bring them out!"

"Vahini?"......

"Yes. What is it?"

"We will miss you .....and your food...and your caring."

She turned her face away, looking towards the kitchen and once again avoided looking at us directly. "Vahini?"

She looked up momentarily, her eyes glazed. She was fighting back tears. Well, if we were getting sentimental and sad about leaving tomorrow, so was she......maybe more so. "Vahini, we will be gone tomorrow, but we will come again. We will come back, for sure. We will never forget you or Haribhau, or anyone for that matter. never!"

"Everyone says they will come back, but no one ever returns once they go. No one. I know, that once you go you will become busy....you have to make your life. For us, life here goes on and we keep waiting and waiting for old friends to return. So many have gone....and you will be gone too. Will you write a letter sometime?" She looked at us with sadness and longing in her eyes.

"Vahini, we are not 'everybody'. We will come back. Promise."

She shrugged, sadness writ large on her face. She dabbed her eyes with the loose end of her sari, and said, "Eat. I hope you enjoy the meal. It's special. I'll come back in the early morning and make tea for you....6 o'clock."

She was gone in a flash, obviously embarrassed by her inadvertent show of emotion. Over the past months we had grown close to her. She really was like a mother/elder sister to us and made our home a home. She cooked us good food and kept us well fed always. She had won our hearts with her tender, loving care and kindness. She had a heart of gold. She was a selfless lady whose only intention was to serve and make others happy.

The meal was delicious and we lapped up the last morsel. Our conversation over the meal was light and superfluous. The truth was, nobody had the courage to say it, but everyone was sad especially after Vahini's teary departure.

After dinner we chatted for a while. The same things were on our minds....try as we would, to break free from thoughts of the impending future, the mind would return to the same old thought and fill us with anxiety. With these conflicting emotions playing truant in our minds we decided to sleep. Tomorrow was an early day.

71. Fare Thee Well. Jawhar!

At 5am my eyes opened without any alarm clock or wake up call. I eased myself out of the bed and stretched and took some deep breaths. The climate was very cold and it was an ordeal to get out of bed. I stepped on the floor tentatively and went to the main door to look out. I was greeted by a rude blast of cold air and semi-darkness. The street light in the distance cast a light that was muted by the thick mist that hung low over Jawhar. The smell of cold village air held a very deep significance in my mind. The silence, the cold and the blurred village landscape bathed in the sole streetlight muted by mist was a scene which the heart captured forever. I stood there, speechless and awe struck at the divine atmosphere just outside our door.

When the cold hit my bones, making me shudder involuntarily, I retreated into the room. I began to wash up and started getting ready to leave. Dadan and Hiroo were just rising too. I was ready by the time Vahini knocked on our door. I opened the door for her and smiled in greeting. She smiled back despite being bundled up in a blanket for warmth.

"Vahini, ek first-class, garam chaha banav. It's so cold. I could do with a hot cup of tea."

Vahini smiled, "Detey! Giving!"

Very soon we were all ready and the tea was also almost done. We all settled at the table in the anteroom. "Bags packed? Anything pending?"

"Nothing!"

Tea was such a welcome drink against the cold. I picked up my cup and holding it with both hands to warm my hands, I settled on the doorstep. Hema would come as soon as she saw someone sitting on the steps. Just as I was taking in the ambience for the last time, she came trotting faithfully with tail wagging and sat down close to me. Her fur against my leg felt so supremely affectionate. I patted her on her forehead, neck and held her close. "We will miss you, my dear." She just kept wagging her tail. Maybe she had an inkling that today was a different day and there was a 'forever' element somewhere.

At 6.30 am we were all set to leave and the time to go had finally arrived. The sadness sat heavy in our hearts. We cast a glance around as if trying to etch the memory of every fine detail for future retrieval. As we got up to leave and Hiroo was putting the lock on the door of our quarters, Hema got up with her tail between her legs, a doleful look in her eyes. She was sensing something too.

We gathered our bags and started walking towards the front of the hospital. The nurses were all gathered at their station. Neelima, Shinde, Kadrekar and Maushi were all there. We stopped there to exchange farewells and despite our mood we broke into a smile when we saw that Neelima had taken out a bar of chocolate to share with us. She was breaking it into pieces and saying," This is so that you leave from here with a sweet taste in your mouth and a bag load of sweet memories!" So saying, she gave us all a small piece.

"Sisters, we will really miss you all. We hope we can all meet again. Take care." A smile, a light touch, and a warm look was all we needed. There was no room for words.

Just around the corner, near the front arch, Dr. Nisal, Dr. Dhande, Dr. Ujwala. and Mr. Vashani were all standing. We were very pleasantly surprised because we thought it was too early to be able to meet them." We realised that you all are going away for good, so we have come to see you all off."

"Take care, boys. It was wonderful to work with you all. I hope, one day, to see you all shining in your chosen fields. God bless you." We shook hands with Dr. Dhande and Dr. Nisal. He patted us affectionately on the head by way of blessing. We bent over to touch his feet as a traditional gesture to solicit blessings and good wishes from someone your superior. Then it was farewell hand-shakes with Vashani and, of course, Mukne who was waiting in the background silently. After Vashani wished us, we turned to Mukne.

He stepped forward and reached into a bag he was carrying and took out something. I couldn't make out in the semi dark but I could swear and say that it looked like a snake. I was baffled and intrigued, not knowing what he was up to. Having brought it out completely he presented it to me with a huge smile on his face. I stared hard, trying to see what he was holding out for me and smiling so much. Tentatively, I reached out and touched it and then I knew what it was. I broke into a huge smile even as he spoke. "Sir, I made this for you. It is for you as a memory from me." it was the whip that Mukne made from leather and lead. He made it just for me. I was spellbound and overwhelmed."Sir, you can wear it like a belt. I made it to your measure."

"Wow. Mukne! This is the best gift ever. I will never forget you. This....," looking at the whip in my hand, "....will be treasured all my life. I promise I won't break anyone's head with it,......but.......i won't let anyone pull my pants off, you bet!" There were smiles all around.

Finally, Dr Ujwala, who was standing demurely, smiling and waiting to say her farewell to us. "Ma'am, we are sorry if we troubled you. We teased you too much." She was smiling indulgently. "But Ma'am, we love you. We wish you all the happiness."

Pushing back her errant lock of hair in her signature style, smiling broadly, she said, "It was enjoyable working with you boys. I never got teased.....so don't worry. But I'll tell you something. You will all miss me. for sure. Go! My best wishes to you!!"

We looked at the watch. "Hey, the bus will leave in fifteen minutes."

Final goodbyes being said, we started hurrying down the hill. Though the weak rays of the sun had started to appear, the mist still hung thick. As we started down the road, the mist lifted ever so slightly rendering the road visible. We briskly covered the distance down the road to the cross junction. Just before turning into the lane, we cast a look over our shoulder for one last glimpse of the hospital. There, in front of the hospital were our friends, the staff, waving goodbye enthusiastically. The mist had lifted just enough for us to catch a fleeting glimpse and then, slowly, it sank back, even as we looked on, enveloping the hospital, the staff and the entire hill in its shroud. It was as though the curtain had come down at the end of a drama and the spectators could now go home. Hitherto, we were part of the drama, but today as the curtain of mist came down we were the spectators and the unspoken message said. "Go home, dear ones. Another drama awaits you there. We were homeward bound. It was time for 'Goodbye, Jawhar!'

Afterword

THIRTY-FIVE YEARS LATER. In the year 2015.

Having been a consultant for more than thirty years, I had the urge to record some of my experiences and to do something that made a lasting impression on humanity. When I looked back at my life I found there were many periods which were very exciting for me and for those who were with me. Of them, my time spent in Jawhar was the best. So Jawhar has become the subject of this book and the people of Jawhar are the central characters around whom we discovered ourselves and a purpose to our lives.

To back track, after finishing internship I returned to Bombay and fortunately was able to get the last, the eighth, seat in General Medicine to pursue my MD. I had the best teachers, both direct and surrogate. After finishing MD, I started private practice. And in the year 2015, I had completed nearly 30 years of practice.

In these thirty years, the world had changed, and so much water had passed from under the bridge. After so many years, I had the opportunity to return to Jawhar, where I had done some of my best work and met some of my best friends. My heart raced with anticipation and excitement at the thought of returning to the place and the people I loved so much.

With the help of the all-knowing Google I tracked down Mahendrasinh Mukne, the Prince of Jawhar, son of the Maharaja Digvijaysinh Mukne. Mahendrasinh lives in Pune. I learnt from him, with immense sadness, that his father, The Maharaja Digvijaysinh had passed away two years ago. I was filled with remorse and found myself wishing I had initiated this search two years earlier. I could have met him again......but now he was gone.

Mahendrasinh, obviously not the 17-year-old Prince anymore, was now the Maharaja of Jawhar. His mother, Rani Saheba, Smt. Indira Raje Mukne, is well and stays with him in Pune. The nurses are scattered all over and have retired from active work. I have been unable to determine their whereabouts.

Maushi passed away peacefully, after suffering a paralytic stroke, a few months after we left. Another cause for remorse. Dr. Nisal retired from active work and thereafter, I have been unable to locate him. Dr. Dhande, has started practice in a village in the hills around Ghoti, on the way to Nashik.

When I reached Jawhar, I was accosted by mixed feelings. The region had urbanised and that had changed the character of the place where I had worked. There were so many buildings and shops, many more than the time when we worked there. There were so many people, so many vehicles. The people no longer looked simple village folk. They were modern and a tad more prosperous than when I left them. The fresh smell of earth was missing.

A young man, Rajesh Tendulkar, an active social worker and businessman, who was a year old when we were there as interns, received me and was my host for the day. He filled me in on all the news I had lost over the years. Our animated conversation went on ceaselessly through the day till it was time to go.

Through Rajesh, I was able to track Haribhau and was able to meet him. Ironically, I half expected to see the same crinkly-eyed, slim, good-natured, young man who I had left thirty-five years ago, and so, I was surprised to see this wizened, serious and slightly plump man approach me. On looking at him hard, I saw some of the vestiges of the old days. It was a moving moment to meet him after so many years. We hugged like long lost friends.

I asked him to take me home. I said I wanted to meet Vahini. His face fell when I made him this request."What happened, Haribhau?"

He hesitated a bit but then said,"Sudha is not there."

"Not there? What do you mean not there. Where is she?" I asked, curious to know what he meant.

For a few moments he didn't answer. He just stared down at the floor despondently. I looked at him anxiously waiting for an answer. After what felt like an eternity, he spoke. In a choking voice he said, "Sudha is no more. She died last year."

Silence.......

I was too shocked and saddened to respond immediately. I could not only feel his grief and understand the reasons for his having aged all of a sudden, I felt a wave of grief rising within me too, rendering me speechless for a few long moments.

"Died?!" I said in shocked disbelief. "How?" I managed a whisper, "She was so young. How could she go so early. No! That's not right. She can't!" I was ranting to myself, unable to come to grips with this piece of shocking news.

"After Maushi passed away, Sudha became the official midwife at the hospital. She remained in service right till she died. She worked really hard, as she always did. She put everybody's interest before her own," Haribhau went on to tell me.

"Oh! That's great news. So she had a big promotion. She deserved it all along, after all the hard work she had put in."

"Yes. One day, she went to attend this delivery and whilst delivering that patient, she felt a tightness in her chest. She didn't tell us till the baby was out." He paused for breath and to gather his emotions. She then told me that she had had chest pain for a long time on that day. The discomfort was soon unbearable. I told the CMO, but even before he could mobilise his resources, she collapsed and died." He had tears streaming down his face even as he said this to me. I couldn't reconcile with this either. She was young, active, lively.... why! Why!?

All I could do is sit by his side, unable to speak without giving away that I was choking too. Haribhau's tears flowed freely.

We sat in silence for a while, understanding and respecting our mutual grief. I remembered vividly, the last day I had met her. I had promised her that I would come, but I came too late. I had promised her that I would write her a letter, but I never wrote. I had sorely let her down. I had broken all my promises to her. And now, when I had this realisation. she was no more. My sadness deepened immeasurably as I remembered all the things that she did for us and the feelings with which she did those things. She had done for us more than a family member would do. She made our lives easy...very easy. She was selfless!

After our brief interlude Haribhau and I parted. I felt something inside me was gone. I felt I had lost someone my own. My visit had probably rekindled Haribhau's grief all over again. My heart went out to him. Her death was an irreparable loss to all of us.

Haribhau leads a retired life in Jawhar, where he is highly respected for all that he has done for the community. After parting from Haribhau we headed for the hospital.

The hospital looked renovated and very busy. The outside looked clean and painted but the precincts had changed completely.

There were ugly concrete and brick buildings all along the road to the hospital and around the hospital. So many, that the hospital was drowned in the sea of concrete. It no longer stood atop the hill majestically as an edifice of healing. Inside the hospital the decor was modern, smooth tiles and painted walls, bright and shining.

But the patients looked the same. Their numbers were more and their poverty remained the same. Nothing much had changed for them. Their problems were the same....malnutrition and infection.

Their lot was the same over the years despite more money being invested in health care. The money allocated for health care seemed to have been used to purchase instruments and furniture, but not for the development of the Adivasi population with the aim of improving their lot.

I made a trip to Nangarmoda, a village near Jawhar. I was struck by the simplicity of the folk there. Nothing had changed for them save that some of the youth had cell phones and there was a little more electricity than in the old days. The children were still malnourished. The women illiterate and malnourished. Frequent childbirth after early marriage, sickness with no accessibility to the benefits of modern medicine, and a myriad other reasons underscored the lopsided policies of the governing authorities.

The visit to the village and the news of Vahini's death had left me very pensive and melancholy. The drive back home was in silence. The village where I had spent my early youth and learnt so much from the people was still in the throes of backwardness. The urge to do something for them arose and continues to arise. This village, like the millions of hamlets and villages of rural India, continues to get a raw deal even as India surges forward on the road to progress and prosperity. India's progress is for the some to become filthy rich even as half the rest languish below the line of subsistence. The poor are effectively camouflaged in villages which are tucked away in oblivion, far from the glitterati of the highway community.

This book, this memoir, is testimony to their plight. It is a story of rural India raw and unexpurgated. It is the story of the heart of India.

Acknowledgements

In the writing of this book I have received help and encouragement from several people to whom I am indebted. My parents, for pushing me to write when I was young. My wife Tejal, my sons, Karan and Arjun, and my daughters (in-law), Sunaina and Jayshree for being my friendly critics and pushing me to limits beyond my imagination. Their support in this, and all my endeavours has been paramount.

I would like to express my gratitude and appreciation to Valeria Mazarakis, Nandini Patodia, Saurabh Mehta, and Beena Salla, for reading the manuscript and giving me invaluable inputs that have served to bring out the best in me.

I would like to record my special appreciation for Dr. Anam Alwani, a promising young medical graduate aspiring to spend a lifetime in medicine. Her comments spurred me on to finish this book knowing that it had served to inspire the young reader to dedicate some part of her life in the service of the lesser privileged.

I have to thank my friend Michele Tilley and my father (in-law) C. C. Maniar, for having read every chapter in its formative stages and for giving me both critical comments and encouragement throughout the writing of this book.

My sincere thanks go out to my loyal and sincere secretary, Raina Rodrigues, for patiently and painstakingly correcting and printing successive drafts of this book till the final version was ready.

My deepest gratitude to Drs. A. B. Nisal, Dhande and Ujwala Narde, and all the staff and nurses of the Patangsha Cottage

Acknowledgements

Hospital, Jawhar, without whom this story would never have happened. I also owe a debt of gratitude to my fellow interns, Hiroo Motwani, Yogendra Sanghvi, Salauddin Dadan, Hemant Painter and A. R. Syed, who were my soul mates through this experience.

I am indeed, indebted, to the hundreds of patients who were the willing recipients of our medical services and who taught us more about life than any book could. This book is dedicated to all those brave hearts who live below the line of subsistence, yet display exemplary warmth, love, courage and compassion for fellow human brings.

– DR. ANAND GOKANI, MD.
CONSULTANT PHYSICIAN.
MUMBAI.

About the Author

DR. ANAND GOKANI, MD.

Is a Consultant Physician with Diabetes and Metabolic Diseases as a speciality. He practices at the Bombay Hospital and the Breach Candy Hospital in Mumbai.

Dr. Gokani's multifaceted approach to healthcare education is impressive. His lectures and workshops cover a broad spectrum of topics, from the technical aspects of diabetes management to the more philosophical considerations of health and ethics. His role as a visiting faculty member at various educational institutions, including Nursing School of SNDT Women's University, the Institute for Gandhian Studies and the Mahatma Gandhi Institute of Medical Sciences in Wardha, highlights his commitment to integrating traditional values with modern medical practice.

The wide reach of his lectures, both in-person and through online platforms like GetSetUp, indicates his ability to connect with and educate a global audience. His extensive writing on diverse subjects such as nutrition, exercise, and the philosophy of life and death further showcases his depth of knowledge and passion for sharing it.

Dr. Gokani's role as a Trustee at the Bombay Medical Aid Foundation is a testament to his dedication to providing care and support to those in need. The Foundation's commitment to offering financial and medical assistance and running an eye hospital with comprehensive care at competitive rates reflects a deep understanding of the importance of accessible healthcare.

He founded a Palliative Care Ward at the hospital to care for terminally ill patients to give them comfort and dignity in the last months of life. He raised 1.8 crores for a Palliative Care Ward Expansion by 25 beds commissioned recently.

An avid traveller, he writes and reads various subjects and enjoys sports and photography. He has authored a book on The Role of Vegetarian Diet in Health and Disease (presently out of print). He has also compiled a book on pictures and aphorisms titled 'At The Crack Of Dawn'.

He is married and lives in Mumbai. He has two sons, two daughters(-in-law) and three grandsons.

Other book published:
'At The Crack of Dawn' a coffee table book on inspiration.